LIVING *with* PURPOSE

DESTINY IMAGE BOOKS BY MYLES MUNROE

The Principle and Power of Kingdom Citizenship (978-0-7684-0868-3)

Understanding Your Place in God's Kingdom (978-07684-4065-2)

Rediscovering the Kingdom (Expanded Edition) (978-07684-3211-4)

Purpose and Power of Love and Marriage (978-07684-2251-1)

Single, Married, Separated and Life After Divorce (978-07684-2202-3)

Waiting and Dating (978-07684-2157-6)

In Pursuit of Purpose (978-15604-3103-9)

Kingdom Principles (978-07684-2373-0)

The Purpose and Power of Praise and Worship (978-07684-2047-0)

Maximizing Your Potential Expanded Edition (978-07684-2674-8)

Understanding Your Potential (978-15604-3046-9)

Kingdom Parenting (978-07684-2418-8)

Overcoming Crisis (978-07684-3052-3)

Applying the Kingdom (978-07684-2597-0)

the LEGACY *and* WISDOM *of*
DR. MYLES MUNROE

LIVING *with* PURPOSE

devotions for discovering your
GOD-GIVEN POTENTIAL

DESTINY IMAGE® PUBLISHERS, INC.
P.O. Box 310, Shippensburg, PA 17257-0310
"Promoting Inspired Lives."

This book and all other Destiny Image and Destiny Image Fiction books are available at Christian bookstores and distributors worldwide.

Cover design by Eileen Rockwell

For more information on foreign distributors, call 717-532-3040.
Or reach us on the Internet: www.destinyimage.com

ISBN 13 HC: 978-0-7684-0844-7

ISBN 13 TP: 978-0-7684-1103-4

ISBN 13 EBook: 978-0-7684-0983-3

For Worldwide Distribution, Printed in the U.S.A.
1 2 3 4 5 6 7 8 9 10 11 / 20 19 18 17 16

YOU HAVE POTENTIAL

POTENTIAL DEFINED

Now it is God who has made us for this very purpose and has given us the Spirit as a deposit, guaranteeing what is to come.
—2 CORINTHIANS 5:5

It is a tragedy to know that with over five billion people on this planet today, only a minute percentage will experience a significant fraction of their true potential. Perhaps you are a candidate for contributing to the wealth of the cemetery. Your potential was not given for you to deposit in the grave. You must understand the tremendous potential you possess and commit yourself to maximizing it in your short lifetime. What is potential, anyway?

Potential is...dormant ability...reserved power...untapped strength... unused success...hidden talents...capped capability.

All you can be but have not yet become...all you can do but have not yet done...how far you can reach but have not yet reached...what you can accomplish but have not yet accomplished. Potential is unexposed ability and latent power.

Potential is therefore not what you have done, but what you are yet able to do. In other words, what you have done is no longer your potential. What you have successfully accomplished is no longer potential. It is said that unless you do something beyond what you have done, you will never grow or experience your full potential. Potential demands that you never settle for what you have accomplished. One of the great enemies of your potential is success. In order to realize your full potential, you must never be satisfied with your last accomplishment. It is also important that you never let what you *cannot do* interfere with what you *can do.* The greatest tragedy in life is not death, but a life that never realized its full potential. You must decide today not to rob the world of the rich, valuable, potent, untapped resources locked away within you. *Potential never has a retirement plan.*

The Potential Principle

The field is the world, and the good seed
stands for the sons of the kingdom.
—Matthew 13:38

To understand your potential, let us look at one of the most powerful elements in nature—the seed. If I held a seed in my hand and asked you, "What do I have in my hand?" what would you say? Perhaps you would answer what seems to be the obvious—a seed. However, if you understand the nature of a seed, your answer would be *fact* but not *truth*.

The truth is I hold a forest in my hand. Why? Because in every seed there is a tree, and in every tree there is fruit or flowers with seeds in them. And these seeds also have trees that have fruit that have seeds...that have trees that have fruit that have seeds, etc. In essence, *what you see is not all there is. That is potential. Not what is, but what could be.*

God created everything with potential, including you. He placed the seed of each thing within itself (see Genesis 1:12), and planted within each person or thing He created the ability to be much more than it is at any one moment. Thus, everything in life has potential.

Nothing in life is instant. People think miracles are instant, but they really are not. They are just a process that has been sped up. Nothing God created is instant, because God does not operate in the instant. He is a God of the potential principle. Everything begins as potential.

He did not create a ready-made human race—the earth was not given an instant population. God made one person—not a million people. He started with one seed. Then from that one He created another. Then He said to those seeds, "Bless you (that means, 'You have My permission'). Be fruitful and multiply and replenish the earth."

In Adam, God gave the earth a seed with the potential of one... one hundred...one thousand...one million.... The five billion people on the earth today were in that one man's loins. God knew that in Adam and Eve there were enough people to fill the earth. That's the way God works. He knows the potential principle because He introduced it. It is Him.

Don't Settle for What You Have

So we fix our eyes not on what is seen,
but on what is unseen. For what is seen is
temporary, but what is unseen is eternal.
—2 Corinthians 4:18

Potential is always present, waiting to be exposed. It demands that you never settle for what you have accomplished. One of the greatest enemies of your potential is success. God wants you to maximize the potential He has given to you. You are not yet what you are supposed to be—though you may be pleased with what you now are. Don't accept your present state in life as final, because it is just that, a state. Don't be satisfied with your last accomplishment, because there are many accomplishments yet to be perfected. Since you are full of potential, you should not be the same person next year that you are this year.

Never accept success as a lifestyle—it is but a phase. Never accept an accomplishment as the end—it is but a mark in the process. Because you are God's offspring, there are many selves within you that lie dormant, untapped and unused. Your primary problem is that you do not think like God does.

There are many selves within you that lie dormant, untapped and unused.

God is always looking for what is not yet visible. He expects to find inside each person and thing He created more than is evident on the outside. On the other hand, man is often satisfied with what he has—or at least if not satisfied, he thinks there is nothing better. Thus he settles for what he has.

Therein lies the tragedy of life. The minute we begin to settle down and be satisfied with what we have, we lose the possibility of revealing what is really inside us. Too often we die without exploring the gifts, abilities, and successes that lay hidden within us. Our thoughts, ideas, and possibilities are not used. We fail to realize the vast potential that is stored within us. We are like batteries in a radio that is never played—our potential is wasted.

COMPLETE YOUR RACE

...and to know this love that surpasses knowledge—that you may be filled to the measure of all the fullness of God.
—EPHESIANS 3:19

As the time for His crucifixion drew near, Jesus spoke of the potential principle in terms of His life. He compared Himself to a kernel of wheat that falls into the ground and dies (see John 12:23-24). A kernel of wheat, when planted, yields many more kernels. Within Jesus was the potential to bring millions of people to God. Thank God Herod didn't succeed when he tried to wipe out Jesus. If he had, Jesus would have died before He could offer Himself as our atonement. His great purpose in life would have been wasted. The seed of His life was much more than His disciples could see. That one seed had the potential to give life to many.

There was a time early in his ministry when the apostle Paul said, "I'd like to leave." Though he preferred to die and be with Christ, he knew his purpose in life had not been completely fulfilled. There was yet much fruitful labor for him to do. It was necessary for the Church that he continue to live. Thank God Paul did not die. The benefit of his wisdom would have been lost to the early Church and to us. His potential to write Colossians and Ephesians may have been forfeited.

Later, near his death, Paul wrote: "Timothy, I've run the race. I've finished the course. I've kept the faith. I've done the work. My award awaits me. I'm ready to die. Keep working after I'm gone" (see 2 Timothy 4:5-7). Everything in life has the potential to fulfill its purpose. *People who die without achieving their full potential rob their generation of their latent ability.* Many have robbed me—they've also robbed you. *To die with ability is irresponsible.*

WHAT'S IN YOUR PACKAGE?

We have different gifts,
according to the grace given us.
—ROMANS 12:6

Perhaps you are wasting your life doing nothing with all you have. God packaged some things in you for the good of the world—use them. We will never know the wealth God planted in you until you bring it up. There's always something in you that we haven't yet seen because that's the way God thinks. Release your ability before you die. Use the power and strength within you for the good of yourself and others. I believe there are books, songs, art works, businesses, poems, inventions, and investments in you that God intended for my children to enjoy. Don't give up until you have lived out the full extent of your potential, because *you have no right to die with my things.* Don't rob the next generation of the wealth, treasure, and tremendous gifts buried deep within you.

If you want to succeed, strike out on new paths. Don't travel the worn paths of accepted success.

No man can climb beyond the limitations of his own belief.

Every day sends to the grave obscure men and women whom fear prevented from realizing their true and full potential.

Failure is not the absence of success. Failure is the neglect of trying.

What you see is not all there is. There is something in everything.

What you have done is no longer your potential.

Potential is what you can do but have not yet done.

EVERYTHING COMES FROM GOD

Through Him all things were made; without Him nothing was made that has been made.
—JOHN 1:3

Everything in life was created with potential and possesses the potential principle. Creation abounds with potential because the Creator Himself is the potential principle.

When we describe God, we often say He is omnipotent. *Omnipotent* means that *God is always potent.* Made up of two words: *omni,* meaning "always," and *potent,* meaning "full of power," *omnipotent* means that God is potentially everything. He has within Him the potential for all that is, was, or ever will be. He is omni-potent or omnipotent.

Everything that was, and everything that is, was in God. That's a very important concept. Everything that was and is, was in God. We have to start with God. Before God made anything, before He created things, there was only God. So before anything was, God is. God is the root, or source, of all life.

Before anything was, God is.

Before there was time, time was—but it was in God. Before God created a galaxy or the Milky Way, He existed. Before there was a universe or a planetary system with the third planet called earth revolving around the sun—before any of that was—He was.

I wonder what it must have been like when God was just by Himself. Let's try to imagine that for a bit. Here's God. He steps out on nothing to view nothing, for there was nothing except God. And so God is standing on top of nothing, looking at nothing because everything was in Him.

The Bible tells us: "*In the beginning, God...*" That means before there was a beginning, there was God. Therefore, God began the beginning and verse 0 of the first chapter of Genesis might possibly read: In God was the beginning. Everything that is was in God. Everything that has ever been made was made by God.

When we connect Genesis 1:0—in God was the beginning—and John 1:1—in the beginning was the Word, and the Word was with God...He was with God in the beginning—we see that the Word was with God *in* the beginning, not *at* the beginning.

The Invisible Became Visible

By faith we understand that the universe was formed at God's command, so that what is seen was not made out of what was visible.
—Hebrews 11:3

In the beginning, God was pregnant with the universe and all things were made by Him. But how did these things come out of Him? How was the universe formed? All things were formed at God's command. He spat them out—poof! From the invisible came the visible. Things that are seen came from things that were unseen.

God always had everything in Him, but we couldn't see it. All we now see was once in an invisible state. Everything that man has ever seen first existed in an invisible state. (Please note that invisible does not mean nonexistent.)

All the buildings we see and the businesses we frequent—people making money and investing money—all that stuff began as ideas. We couldn't see them because they were in somebody's mind. The stores where we shop, also everything on the shelves and racks in those stores, began as ideas in someone's mind. They didn't exist before, yet they did. Although they weren't present in their current form, they existed as lumber and concrete and nails, cotton and wool and flax, steel and pulleys and motors.

Someone had an idea. Through work they put their idea into things that are visible. Today they take your money.

Everything starts in the invisible state. Everything we now see used to be unseen.

In the beginning there was only God. At creation the entire unseen universe became visible. Everything that has been created was made by the word of God. Although it already existed, God spoke so that what was invisible could become visible. You would never have known it existed, except God spat it out in faith.

By faith God spat out what was in Him. Everything in Him started to come forth. What we now see was birthed by God from what was invisibly within Him. Whatever you see came from the unseen—nothing exists that was not at some time in God. Thus, *faith is not the evidence of things that do not exist. It is the evidence of things that are not yet seen.* Everything we see has always been. It became visible when God spoke it into being. God is the source of life.

YOU ARE NOT JUNK

I praise You because I am fearfully and wonderfully made; Your works are wonderful, I know that full well.
—PSALM 139:14

There are many people who are being passed by because others don't see what is in them. But God has shown me what's in me, and I know it is in you too. My job is to stop you and say: "Can you see what's in you? Do you know your potential? Do you know that you are not just someone born in a ghetto over the hill? There's a wealth of potential in you."

A sculptor sees so differently. They say Michelangelo used to walk around a block of marble for days—just walking around it, talking to himself. First he would see things in the rock; then he would go and take them out.

Insight like that of a sculptor is seen in the Bible. When the world dumps and rejects you, and you land on the garbage heap of the world, God walks along and picks you up. He looks deep within you and sees a person of great worth.

Don't ever let anybody throw you away. You are not junk. When God looks at you, He sees things that everybody else ignores. You are worth so much that Jesus went to Calvary to salvage and reclaim you. The Spirit of God connected to your spirit is the only true judge of your worth. Don't accept the opinions of others because they do not see what God sees.

God Looked and Saw...

All the days ordained for me were written in
Your book before one of them came to be.
—Psalm 139:16

God looked at Adam and saw a world. He looked at Abraham and saw nations. In Jacob, a deceiver, He saw a Messiah. In Moses the murderer, God saw a deliverer. Can you imagine looking at a stammering young man and seeing the greatest leader in history?

God saw a king in a shepherd boy. When the Israelites wanted a king, God sent Samuel to the home of Jesse. All the sons of Jesse twirled out before Samuel, from the greatest to the least. Finally, after Jesse had paraded all of his sons before him, Samuel said, "I'm sorry. None of these is God's choice for king. Do you have any other sons?"

Then Jesse said, "Yes...well no. I just remembered. I do have a little boy, my youngest son. He's just a little runt who's out taking care of the sheep."

"Bring him," Samuel replied. "Let me look at him."

So Jesse sent for his youngest son. When Samuel saw Jesse's youngest son walk into the house, a little boy, he began to unscrew the lid of his vase. "I think I have found the guy I'm looking for," Samuel said. (Notice that God chose the son who was out working. He was busy. God chooses busy people.)

Most of us are like Jesse. We look, but we don't see. Were you the black sheep in your family? (You know God likes sheep.) Has your family told you that you are a nobody? Have you been put off and put out and told so many times that you will amount to nothing that you have begun to believe it? Do you *feel* like the black sheep?

You are probably the one God is waiting for in the house. God sees things deep within you that others can't see. They look at you and see a nobody; God looks at you and sees a worthwhile somebody. You may spend your whole life competing with others—trying to prove that you are somebody—and still feel like nobody. Be free from that today! You do not have to live with that any longer. You don't have to *try* to be somebody, because you are somebody.

YOU CAME OUT OF GOD

Then God said, "Let us make man in Our image, in Our likeness....
—GENESIS 1:26

Not only are all things composed of that from which they came, they must also remain attached to that source in order to live. All things must be maintained and sustained by where they came from. The minute a plant decides it doesn't like the earth anymore, it dies. The minute the fish decide they are tired of water, they die. The minute animals decide, "We don't want to eat any more dirt," they begin to die.

Thus, whatever God created came from that to which He spoke. All things were created by God's word to a source. The source of the creation also becomes, then, the essence of that creation. All things are composed of whatever they came from and hence contain the potential of that source. That means plants only have the potential of the soil. Animals only have the potential of dirt.

All things are composed of whatever they came from and hence contain the potential of that source.

When God wanted fish, He spoke to the water. When He wanted animals, He spoke to the dirt. When God created human beings, He spoke to Himself.

> *Then God said, "Let Us make man in Our image, in Our likeness...." So God created man in His own image, in the*

> *image of God He created him; male and female He created them* (Genesis 1:26-27).

God created you by speaking to Himself. You came out of God and thus bear His image and likeness.

God Has a Book on You

Before a word is on my tongue you know it completely, O Lord.
—Psalm 139:4

God designed you to be somebody. He looked at your unformed body and declared, "This child is good." All His plans for your life were set out long before you took a breath. He wrote out the order of your days before you lived even one day (see Psalm 139:16). There's a book on you. Some chapters God wrote about you haven't even been touched yet.

Some of you are playing around in the index or you have spent years in the table of contents. Perhaps you are 30 years old and you still don't know God's plan for your life. That's playing around on the contents page. You are 30 years old and still wondering what you are supposed to be. You haven't even started yet.

Others have jumped ahead of God's plan. Though His design calls for you to be married in chapter 17, you got married in chapter 2. You have ignored the things God wanted you to learn and experience in chapters 2 through 16 so you would be prepared for marriage in chapter 17. You have missed out on many experiences and discoveries because you moved ahead of God's schedule.

Some people are so busy peeking into chapter 17 they don't have time to live chapters 2 and 3 and 4.... Or perhaps you have pulled chapter 17 into chapter 2 so that the rest of the book is destroyed. You will never have the opportunity to experience all the chapters if you pull parts of later chapters into the early ones.

KNOCK THE LIMITS OFF YOUR LIFE

Jesus looked at them and said, "With man this is impossible, but with God all things are possible."
—MATTHEW 19:26

The concept of Mark chapter 11 is that if you ask anything—if you can believe what you desire hard enough—God says it will be done. Somehow God gives us a little glimpse into our potential. He comes into our situation as if He's disturbed. God is disappointed in the human race. It's almost as though God looks at the ideas He stored in us and says with a voice of disappointment, "If you only knew what you can do." That's the attitude of God toward you and me. God is totally disappointed in us because He knows what we can do. But we don't. And so He says to us: "All things are possible if you'd just believe, dummy." He's always knocking the limits off our lives.

Too often we are not willing to *believe* like God defines believe. God does not say, "Everything is possible if you get the idea." Things don't become reality because we have an idea. We have to believe in the idea. We have to believe we can do it by committing ourselves to it—abandoning ourselves to it—even if it costs us our lives. That's what it takes to believe in the Lord Jesus Christ—to lose our lives…to abandon ourselves. We must say, "I'm going to go into eternity believing in Jesus. I'm not sure what's out there, but I'm going to ride on that Name and that atonement."

God isn't impressed by your dreams. Most of us never wake up long enough to do anything with our dreams. You may have great dreams for your life, but you prefer to stay asleep because when you wake up reality says, "OK, let's get to work." It's easier to dream an idea than to work it out. Everything is possible if you will abandon yourself to an idea enough that you are willing to lose your life for it. Thinking is great. But all things are possible when we *believe.* Jesus said in Mark chapter 11, "Whatever you *desire* when you pray, believe you'll receive it, and you will have it." The word *desire* is the key. Being interested in or attracted to something is not desiring it. To *desire* means "to crave for something at the expense of losing everything."

God's work in creation began with a plan. God conceived in His mind what He wanted before speaking His creations into visible form. By the time God was ready to speak, it was just a matter of taking what was in the plan and putting it on the site.

You Can Do All Things

I can do everything through Him who gives me strength.
—Philippians 4:13

The apostle Paul, when looking back over his years in the Lord's service, stated that he could do all things through Christ who strengthens him. The Greek terminology for strengthen does not mean we are weak and God comes and props us up. Paul's words literally mean: "Christ who continues to infuse me with ability." Thus Paul is saying: "I can do all things through the potential of Christ who infuses me with the ability to do all things." This strength is not a strength that comes once in a while, but a continual ability that is infused into us because we are connected to Christ. Thus our potential is not limited to doing *some* of the things God asks us to do. We can do *all things*—whatever we believe and desire to do for God. We can do this because the ability to do so is already deposited in us. The basis for this deposit of Christ's ability goes back to God's work in creation.

God is the source of all potential because everything that is was in God. He created everything with potential and gave it the ability to fulfill itself. The potential God gave is related to the source from which He took the thing. That means whatever you came out of is an indication of your potential. Thus your potential is as great as God's potential, because when God wanted you, He spoke to Himself. When He wanted plants and animals, God spoke to the ground. But when He wanted human beings, God spoke to Himself. You came out of God. Thus the limit of your potential is God.

GOD'S WORD ON YOUR POTENTIAL—PART 1

Without faith it is impossible to please God....
—HEBREWS 11:6

You have the potential to be in God's class.

> *So God created man in His own image; in the image of God He created him; male and female He created them* (Genesis 1:27).

God sees you as being in His class. Because He made you in His image, you have the potential to be in the God class—which is spirit.

You have the potential to operate like God.

> *Then God said, "Let Us make man in Our image, in Our likeness..."* (Genesis 1:26).

When God made you in His likeness, He did not make you to *look* like Him. He made you to *function* like Him. That's what *likeness* literally means. When God created you, He made you to operate like Him. If you are not functioning like God, you are "malfunctioning," because God wired and designed you to function like Him. How does God function? His Word says, "*Without faith it is impossible to please God*" (Hebrews 11:6). God functions by faith. You and I were designed to operate by faith. Our potential therefore needs faith in order to be maximized.

God sees in you the potential to dominate, rule and subdue the whole earth.

> *[God said] "...let them rule over the fish of the sea and the birds of the air, over the livestock, over all the earth, and over all the creatures that move along the ground."...God blessed them and said to them "...Rule over the fish of the sea and the birds of the air and over every living creature that moves on the ground"* (Genesis 1:26,28).

God created you to rule over all the earth and everything that creeps in it. He will never demand anything of you He didn't already build into you. Thus, if the earth in any way is dominating you, you are malfunctioning. You were not created to give into cigarettes or submit to alcohol. God did not intend for you to be controlled by drugs, sex, money, power, or greed. If any of these are governing you, you are living below your privilege. Because God has already declared it to be so, you have the ability to dominate the earth. Everything in the earth must be under your subjection, not mastering you.

GOD'S WORD ON YOUR POTENTIAL—PART 2

For the word of the Lord is right and true;
He is faithful in all He does.
—PSALM 33:4

You have the ability to be fruitful and reproduce after your kind.

God blessed them and said to them, "*Be fruitful and increase in number; fill the earth and subdue it*" (Genesis 1:28).

Again God is calling forth something that's already in you. He didn't tell the man and the woman to *try* to be fruitful, He simply told them to *do* it. He knew they already had the ability to multiply and reproduce and fill the earth. You too can reproduce yourself. He always places the potential inside before He calls it forth. Whatever God calls you to do, He has already built in.

You have the ability to imagine and plan to do anything.

> *The Lord said, "If as one people speaking the same language they have begun to do this, then nothing they plan to do will be impossible for them"* (Genesis 11:6).

God gave you the ability to imagine and plan and bring into being anything you desire. Now if you read this passage in its entirety, the people to whom God was talking had planned to build a tower. God didn't stop them from building a tower by cutting off their potential. He stopped them by confusing their language, because He couldn't stop their potential.

You have the same potential God saw in those people. If you decide to do something, and you believe in it hard enough and commit yourself to work for it long enough, nothing in the universe can stop you. That's what God is saying. If you want to do anything, God already said, "You can do it." Only if you lack the commitment to follow after your dream will your dream remain unfinished. The potential to do and plan anything is in you if you will believe and persevere.

You have the potential to believe impossibilities into possibilities.

> ...*Everything is possible for him who believes* (Mark 9:23).

Not only are you able to plan, but you also have the ability to believe something that seems impossible and actually make it possible. If you can abandon yourself to an idea and sacrifice all you have for that idea, God says, "It's possible for that idea to come to pass."

GOD'S WORD ON YOUR POTENTIAL—PART 3

Your word, O Lord, is eternal; it stands firm in the heavens.
—PSALM 119:89

You have the potential to influence physical and spiritual matter.

> *I will give to you the keys of the kingdom of Heaven; whatever you bind on earth will be bound in Heaven, and whatever you loose on earth will be loosed in Heaven* (Matthew 16:19).

Jesus is talking here about your power to influence what's on earth as well as what's in Heaven. If you bind something on earth, it will be bound in Heaven. You have influence in Heaven. Likewise, if you loose something on earth, Heaven has to do the same thing—loose it. You have the power to influence things in both realms of earth and Heaven.

You have the potential to receive whatever you ask.

> *If you remain in Me and My words remain in you, ask whatever you wish, and it will be given you* (John 15:7).

God says you have the potential to receive whatever you ask. That's frightening. You have a blank check—but there is one condition on the cashing of that check: You must abide in Christ, and His words must abide in you. If that condition is met, you can ask anything in Jesus' name and it will be done for you. Jesus wants to knock the limits off your mind. But first He requires that you stay hooked up with God. Then He says, "Go ahead and ask me for anything. I'll do whatever you ask." What potential! That's God's word on *you*.

You have the potential to do greater works than Jesus did.

> *I tell you the truth, anyone who has faith in Me will do what I have been doing. He will do even greater things than these, because I am going to the Father* (John 14:12).

Jesus sees in you the potential to do greater things than He did. If Jesus says you have that potential, it's in there somewhere. Remember, whatever God says, you can do. He won't ask you to do anything He hasn't already wired you to do.

God believes in you. He knows the vastness of your potential. If He gives you an assignment, He's already given you the ability to fulfill what He asks. Along with His *demand* always comes the *capability* to meet that demand. But remember: To release your potential, you must be related to your Source. Only as you are connected to God, can you fulfill and maximize your true potential.

SAY "YES" TO JESUS

May the grace of the Lord Jesus Christ, and the love of God, and the fellowship of the Holy Spirit be with you all.
—2 CORINTHIANS 13:14

Sin, or rebellion against God, clogs up our potential. Disobedience to God may have stunted your capacity for growth. But God sees and cares about that problem. He sent Jesus into the world to die for you. Jesus doesn't have a problem knowing who He is and what He can do. *You* have that problem. Jesus came to die so you can know who you are and what is the fullness of *your* potential. He came to open up the capacity of who you are—to unclog your true self.

Calvary is God's way of providing the means to unplug your true potential. Because disobedience has capped off your potential, God offers you forgiveness and hope through Jesus Christ. In your plugged up state, you can't begin to touch your true ability. Only after you say "yes" to Jesus (and your spirit begins to communicate and fellowship again with the Holy Spirit) can you start the journey of fulfilling all the potential God planted within you before you were born.

It is my earnest desire that you will realize the awesome wealth of potential residing in you. But more important than this potential is the necessity that you understand your need for a personal relationship with Your Creator through the agency He has provided, Jesus Christ.

I encourage you to pray the following prayer with me in faith:

> *Dear heavenly Father, Creator and Manufacturer of my life, today I submit my life to You, totally surrendering the product of my whole life to You for complete repair, maintenance and renewal in Jesus Christ. I confess Him as the only Savior of my life and submit to Him as my Lord. By faith I this moment receive the Holy Spirit, who, by His power, makes me an eternal citizen of Your Kingdom of Heaven. I commit myself to serve and acknowledge You in all my ways as I endeavor to maximize my potential for Your praise and glory.*
>
> *This I pray in Jesus' Name, Amen.*

TEN KEYS TO RELEASING YOUR POTENTIAL—PART 1

His divine power has given us everything we need for life and godliness through our knowledge of Him who called us by His own glory and goodness.
—2 PETER 1:3

His divine power has given us everything we need for life and godliness through our knowledge of God.

Here are first five keys to releasing your full potential.

Key #1—You must know (be related to) your Source.

The *warranty/guarantee* agreement is set by the manufacturer if he is to take responsibility for the maximum performance, maintenance, and servicing of the product.

The same relationship exists between *God* and *man.* God guarantees the maximum performance of our potential if we submit to the conditions, specifications, and standards set by Him.

Key #2—You must understand how the product was designed to function.

Every manufacturer designs, develops, and produces his product to function in a specific manner.

God created man and designed him to function like He does—*by faith and love.* Our potential cannot be released without faith and love. Fear and hatred cause the short circuit of our potential.

Key #3—You must know your purpose.

Every product exists for a specific purpose.

God created you and gave you birth for a purpose. Purpose gives birth to responsibility, and responsibility makes demands on potential.

Key #4—You must understand your resources.

All manufacturers provide access to the necessary resources for the proper maintenance, sustenance, and operation of their products.

God provided for human beings tremendous material and physical resources to sustain and maintain us as we proceed in realizing, developing, and maximizing our potential.

Key #5—You must have the right environment.

Environment consists of the conditions that have a direct or indirect effect on the performance, function, and development of a thing.

God created everything to flourish within a specific environment. The fall of man contaminated his environment and poisoned the atmosphere of our potential. The key to releasing your true potential is the restoration of God's original environment. Jesus came to restore us to the Father. He sent the Holy Spirit to restore our internal environment.

TEN KEYS TO RELEASING YOUR POTENTIAL—PART 2

Therefore, my dear friends, as you have always obeyed—not only in my presence, but now much more in my absence—continue to work out your salvation with fear and trembling.
—PHILIPPIANS 2:12

Here are the remaining keys to releasing your full potential.

Key #6—You must work out your potential.

Potential is dormant ability. But ability is useless until it is given responsibility.

Work is a major key to releasing your potential. Potential must be exercised and demands made on it, otherwise it will remain potential. Good ideas do not bring success. To release your true potential, you must be willing to work.

Key #7—You must cultivate your potential.

Potential is like a seed. It is buried ability and hidden power that need to be cultivated. You must feed your potential the fertilizer of good positive company, give it the environment of encouragement, pour out the water of the Word of God, and bathe it in the sunshine of personal prayer.

Key #8—You must guard your potential.

With all the wealth of your potential, you must be careful to guard and protect it. The Bible calls your potential a *treasure* in earthen vessels. You must guard your visions and dreams from sin, discouragement, procrastination, failures, opinions, distractions, traditions, and compromise.

Key #9—You must share your potential.

God created the entire heavens and earth with the potential principle, which can only be fulfilled when it is shared. True potential and fulfillment in life is not what is accomplished, but who benefits from them. Your deposit was given to enrich and inspire the lives of others.

Key #10—You must know and understand the laws of limitation.

Freedom and power are two of the most important elements in our lives. Potential is the essence of both. Potential is power. But freedom needs law to be enjoyed, and power needs responsibility to be effective. God has set laws and standards to protect our potential and to secure our success. Obedience is protection for potential.

All of these keys and principles are proven throughout human history to be true. Any violation of these laws limits the release and maximization of your potential. Commit yourself to obeying the Manufacturer. Then watch your life unfold as you discover the hidden ability that was always within you.

THE PRINCIPLE OF CAPACITY

I know that when I come to you, I will come in
the full measure of the blessing of Christ.
—ROMANS 15:29

The true capacity of a product is determined not by the user but the manufacturer. An automobile is built with the capacity to travel at 180 mph; therefore its full potential was determined by the manufacturer. The true potential of the car is not affected by my opinion of its ability or by my previous experience with driving. Whether or not I use the full capacity of the car's engine does not reduce its potential capacity.

The same principle applies to your life. God created you like He did everything else, with the capacity to fulfill your purpose. Therefore, your true capacity is not limited, reduced, or altered by the opinion of others or your previous experience. You are capable of attaining the total aptitude given to you by your Creator to fulfill His purpose for your life. Therefore, *the key to maximizing your full potential is to discover the purpose or reason for your life and commit to its fulfillment at all cost.*

The apostle Paul, in a letter to the church at Corinth, spoke of the hidden secret wisdom of our destiny that is invested in each of us by our Creator God.

> *No, we speak of God's secret wisdom, a wisdom that has been hidden and that God destined for our glory before time began. None of the rulers of this age understood it, for if they had,*

> *they would not have crucified the Lord of glory. However, as it is written: "No eye has seen, no ear has heard, no mind has conceived what God has prepared for those who love Him"* (1 Corinthians 2:7-9).

The implication in verse 9 is that no human has the right or the ability to fully determine or measure the capacity of the potential you possess.

GO FOR IT!

Whatever your hand finds to do, do it with all your might, for in the grave, where you are going, there is neither working nor planning nor knowledge nor wisdom.
—ECCLESIASTES 9:10

I am convinced that our Creator never intended for us to be normal—that is, to get lost in the crowd of "the norm." This is evidenced by the fact that among the 5.8 billion people on this planet, no two individuals are alike; their fingerprints, genetic code, and chromosome combinations are all distinct and unique. In reality, God created all people to be originals, but we continue to become copies of others. Too often we are so preoccupied with trying to fit in, that we never stand out.

You were designed to be distinctive, special, irreplaceable, and unique, so refuse to be "normal"! Go beyond average! Do not strive to be accepted, rather strive to be yourself. Shun the minimum; pursue the maximum. Utilize all your functions—maximize yourself! Use yourself up for the glory of your Creator. *I admonish you: Die empty. Die fulfilled by dying unfilled.*

This book is written for the "normal" person who wishes to exceed the norm. It is for the "ordinary" individual who has determined to be "extra-ordinary." It is for the individual just like you who knows that somewhere deep inside, there is still so much you have not released: so much yet to do, so much left to expose, so much to maximize.

Live life with all your might; give it all you have. Do it until there is nothing left to do because you have become all you were created to be, done all you were designed to do, and given all you were sent to give. Be satisfied with nothing less than your best.

WHERE YOUR POTENTIAL IS FOUND

Get Out the Clog

His master replied, "Well done, good and faithful servant! You have been faithful with a few things; I will put you in charge of many things. Come and share your master's happiness!."
—Matthew 25:21

The Bible tells a story about talents and potential. The talents in the story are symbols of the vast store of abilities our Creator has planted within us. In the story, the master of the estate entrusts some of his wealth to three of his servants. The first man invests his talent and doubles the wealth the master had entrusted to his care. The second servant also doubles what the master had given him. With them the master is very pleased. Finally the master turns to the third servant and asks, "What have you done with your talent?"

The servant answered, "I was afraid to misuse the talent, so I carefully hid it. Here it is. I am giving it back to you in the same condition that I received it."

In fury the master rebuked his servant, "You wicked and lazy servant. How dare you not use the gifts I gave to you?"

The master then said, "Take my money from him and throw this useless fellow into the street."

We are responsible for the potential stored within us. We must learn to understand it and effectively use it. Too often our successes prevent us from seeking that which yet lies within us. Success becomes our enemy as we settle for what we have. Refuse to be satisfied with your last accomplishment, because potential never has a retirement plan. Do not let what you *cannot* do interfere with what you *can* do. In essence, what you see is not all there is.

YOU CAN DO EVERYTHING GOD ASKS

...and His incomparably great power for us who believe.
That power is like the working of His mighty strength.
—EPHESIANS 1:19

God is good. He has built into you the potential to produce everything He calls for. When God says, "Love your enemies," don't start listing reasons why you can't. The ability to love is built in...it's there...no excuses. God wouldn't ask for it if it wasn't available. He wired you to produce everything He demands.

God also wired everything else to produce what He demands from it. God looks at a piece of fruit and says, "In you there is a tree. There is a seed in you, and that seed is a tree. It's there, and I demand what I put in." So God says, "Plant that seed and a tree has to come out; I put a tree in that seed. Before you were given the fruit, I made the seed with the tree." That's the way God thinks. Hallelujah!

Whenever God gives you a responsibility, He also gives you the ability to meet that responsibility. In other words, *whatever God calls for, He provides for.* If God tells you to do something, He knows you can do it. So don't you dare tell God that you can't. Just because He told you to assume that responsibility means He knows you can do it. The problem isn't that you can't, it's just that you *won't.*

Whether you use the ability God has deposited within you is totally up to you. How well you assume the responsibilities God gives you is not so much a question of how much you *do*, but rather how much of the available power you use. What you are doing is not near what your ability is. What you have accomplished is a joke when compared with what you could accomplish—you are not working enough with the power of God (emphasis on work).

If You Think It, You Can Do It

There is surely a future hope for you, and
your hope will not be cut off.
—Proverbs 23:18

You have a deposit of God's ability! Any person who sets a limit on what he *can* do, also sets a limit on what he *will* do. No one can determine how much you can produce except you and God. So there is nothing in this world that should stop you from accomplishing and realizing and fulfilling and maximizing your full potential.

Proverbs 23:7 tells us: If you can conceive it, you can do it. Obviously God is trying to communicate that you *can* do anything you can *think*. If you can conceive it, the fact that you can conceive it means you can do it. It doesn't matter if it's never been done—if you think it, you can do it. Likewise, if you never think it, you can't do it. God allows you to think only what you can do. If He doesn't allow you to think it, He knows you can't do it.

Think about the things you've been thinking recently. The fact that you thought them means you can do them. Now don't get me wrong. Thinking doesn't get it done. Thinking implies you can do it. See yourself doing the thing in your thoughts. Make your thought into an idea, and your idea into an imagination. Take that imagination and document it into a plan. Then go to it (of course with the proper rest periods). Put your plan into action. If you thought it, you can do it.

If God Has It, You Have It

But the fruit of the Spirit is love, joy, peace, patience, kindness, goodness, faithfulness, gentleness and self-control.
—Galatians 5:22-23

Each of the fruit of the Spirit is an attribute of God. God unconditionally says, "They are you." God knows you have love. He knows you have joy—it doesn't matter what you are going through. God knows you have joy down there inside you, because Christ is joy.

Peace. How do you explain that? I used to think the Prince of Peace. "Hello, Prince." I always thought: "Others have the peace. Give me some, Jesus." But that's not what the Bible teaches. The Bible says you have peace. When you are unhappy and everything is going wrong, God says, "Have peace." He doesn't say, "I'll give you some peace," because He can't give you what you already have. Peace is not a gift; it's a fruit. Joy is not a gift; it's a fruit. If God has it, you have it.

In the beginning there was only God. All that is and all that was, was in God—everything. We came out of God. Thus, everything that is in God, is in us: love…joy…peace…patience…kindness… goodness…faithfulness…gentleness…self-control. These are in God and in us.

"Love? I can't like that person."

"You're lying to me," God says. "What do you mean you can't love? Your spirit connected to My Spirit can do all things. Since I love, you can too."

As Romans 5:5 puts it: "...*God has poured out His love into our hearts by the Holy Spirit*...." After you return to God, the Holy Spirit brings love back to your heart. He ignites the stuff that has been in your heart all along. It's not that you *can't* love; you just don't *want* to love. Love isn't a decision you make, because you already have it. That's why you can love your enemies.

How High Can You Jump?

Therefore I tell you, whatever you ask for in prayer, believe that you have received it, and it will be yours.
—Mark 11:24

The people who are blessings to humanity are usually men and women who decide there is more to them than what other people have said. People who bless the world are people who believe there is an ability inside them to accomplish something that has never been done. Though they may not know *exactly* what they can do, they *try* because they believe they can accomplish something.

I remember the day I found out that I could jump really high—about 8 feet high.

There was a lady who lived behind our house from whose fruit trees we would occasionally feast and help ourselves. When we were little kids, we would crawl under the fence. One day while I was on her side of the fence, her very vicious dog suddenly appeared. I had just touched down after climbing the fruit tree. As I carefully considered the distance between the fence, the dog, and myself, I knew I had to make a run for it. I ran toward the fence with the dog close behind me. As the fence came closer and closer, all I could say was "O God, I'm dead." All I could think was "jump." As I left the ground, my heart was pounding and my chest felt like an arcade full of shouting people. I was so afraid! When I landed, I was safely on the other side of the fence.

I thank God for that dog. He was a blessing in my life. I never jumped that high before, and I never have since, but at least I know that I did it. I discovered that day there is a lot more potential in me than I realized was there.

The same is true for you. You aren't doing more because no one has challenged you. I want to take you from the realm of waiting for people to challenge you and encourage you to challenge yourself. Don't just look at life and say, "Well, I'm going to wait until a demand is made on me and then I will produce." Make a demand on yourself. Say to yourself, "Look, I am going to become the best in this area no matter what people have done before me." Then go after that. You will accomplish it if you set out to do it.

TELL ME TO COME

If anyone serves, he should do it with the strength God provides, so that in all things God may be praised through Jesus Christ. To Him be the glory and the power for ever and ever. Amen.
—1 PETER 4:11

I am reminded of a young fisherman who decided, "I'm going to take a chance and try to walk on water." One night as the disciples were crossing Lake Galilee it was hard rowing. They were being tossed about by the waves because the wind was against them. As they struggled, a man came toward them, walking on the water. In fear they cried out, "It's a ghost." Only when He spoke to them did the disciples recognize that it was Jesus. Peter then said, "*Lord, if it's you...tell me to come to you on the water*" (Matthew 14:28). And when Jesus said "Come!" Peter had the guts to respond to Jesus' order.

I believe every one of those disciples could have walked on water. The potential was in them even as it was in Peter. But only Peter succeeded, because only Peter had the guts to say, "If you challenge me, I'll take your challenge." Although we may laugh or criticize Peter for sinking, none of us has ever walked on water. He's the only guy who can say in Heaven when we get there, "I walked on water. What did you do?"

Everybody sees Jesus, but very few of us ask Jesus, "Tell me something to do. Give me something to challenge my potential." Men and women who are assets to the world and bring change for the better are those who give their potential something to maximize. *Give your ability a responsibility*; that would change the world. There is a wealth of ability in you, but you haven't given it any responsibility. Don't die without maximizing your ability—that's irresponsible. You have no right to die with what God put in you to live out.

DEMAND SOMETHING OF YOUR POTENTIAL

With this in mind, we constantly pray for you, that our God may count you worthy of His calling, and that by His power He may fulfill every good purpose of yours and every act prompted by your faith.
—2 THESSALONIANS 1:11

After God created Adam, He gave him a job. God knew Adam's potential to name all the animals would never be released unless it was challenged. Potential must be exercised to be fulfilled. Demands must be made on potential if it is to be released and fulfilled. God has given you potential. Unless you make demands on it, you will die with it. Unless you venture to try things you've never done before, you'll never experience the wealth that lives within you. Decide today, "I'm going to do something I've never done before." "I'm going to get a promotion this year in my job." "I'm going to win more people to Jesus this year than my church and my pastor ever did." If you have a business, resolve to cut the overhead and increase service. Give your potential some demands. It needs to be maximized and challenged.

The greatest works in the world will be done by people who don't care who gets the credit. I don't want to be famous, I just want to be faithful. I don't want to be well known, I want to be well used. I don't want to be powerful, I want to be potent. Success requires striking out on new paths instead of traveling those that are well worn. Genius is 1 percent inspiration and 99 percent perspiration. There are many people with great ideas, but they have no desire to try. There are four steps to the accomplishment of your dream: Prepare prayerfully. Plan purposefully. Proceed positively. Pursue persistently. Failure is the path of least persistence.

SOURCE DETERMINES POTENTIAL

For in Him you have been enriched in every way—
in all your speaking and in all your knowledge.
—1 CORINTHIANS 1:5

Everything God creates has the same components as its source. Wherever something comes from determines it components. Or to say it another way: Everything is made up of the same stuff as what it came out of. Therefore plants are made up of 100 percent dirt. They consist of the same things as the dirt. Animals also are one hundred percent dirt, or whatever is in the soil.

So when a plant dies, it goes back to where it came from—you can't find it. When an animal dies, it goes back to where it came from—you can't find it. When man dies, he goes back to the spirit realm.

So whatever something comes from determines the components of which it is made. And whatever something comes from determines its potential. *Potential is related to source.* A plant can be no more than the dirt can be. Likewise, animals can be no more than the dirt can be. Since you came out of God, you have the same components as God and your potential is determined by God.

Wherever something comes from, it has to remain attached to where it came from in order to fulfill itself. All created things must be maintained by their source. Thus plants need soil to live. They can't live without the dirt. If a plant decides, "I'm tired of the soil," it also decides "I'm ready to die." Therefore, if you decide you don't need God, you have also decided never to become all you are capable of being. The potential of everything is related to source; everything must be attached to its source if it is going to fulfill its potential.

Our life depends upon our Source. We came out of God and contain a measure of His ability. But our only hope of fulfilling that ability lies in God. We must be hooked up with God if we are going to tap any of our true potential. Jesus came to bring us back to God so God's original intention when He took man out of Himself could be fulfilled. Thus the key to your full potential is staying related to God.

THE SOURCE OF ALL POTENTIAL IS IN THE OMNIPOTENT ONE

...far above all rule and authority, power and dominion, and every title that can be given, not only in the present age but also in the one to come.
—EPHESIANS 1:21

Principle: The potential of a thing is related to its source. This means wherever something comes from determines the potential it has. The degree or potency of that potential can be measured by the demands made on it by the one who made it. Therefore, the potential or ability of a thing is determined by the purpose for which the creator, manufacturer or maker made it. Every product is designed and engineered by the manufacturer to fulfill its purpose. Therefore its potential is built in. The purpose establishes the demands to be placed on the product, and the demands determine its potential.

This principle is evidenced by all manufacturers who enclose a *manual* with their product detailing the expected performance and potential of their product. The manufacturer wants you to read the manual before using the product so it can tell you what demands to make on the product. They are confident you can make those demands because they have already built into the product the necessary components to fulfill the demands. The potential of a thing is therefore not determined by opinions, assumptions or prejudices, but only by the demands placed on it by the one who made it.

Your true ability and potential should not be measured by the limitations of an academic test or an Intelligence Quotient score. Nor should it be determined by the social, cultural, economic and educational "norms" of your society. Society did not create you. You are not a product of your culture. You are not the offspring of your economy. You were not created by the Department of Education. Therefore, none of these has the right to determine how much potential you really possess. If you want to know how much potential you have, first discover who created or manufactured you. Then check the demands He is making upon your life. Whatever He is demanding of you, *you can do.*

FROM REVELATION TO INFORMATION—FROM DISCERNMENT TO SENSE

Since we live by the Spirit, let us keep in step with the Spirit.
—GALATIANS 5:25

Man's original state in the garden of Eden, before the fall, was one of perfect union and fellowship with God. He was designed to live from the *inside* to the *outside*, from his *spirit* to his *body*. God designed man to be *led* by his spirit, not *driven* by his environment. Man was intended to live through spiritual *discernment*, not physical *senses*. But when Adam (the first man) disobeyed God, he destroyed his fellowship and communion with the Spirit of God (see Genesis 3). The consequence was death.

Death is isolation from the spirit world of God. Through disobedience, man's spirit lost contact with the Source of Heaven. As a result, man became a victim of his *soul* (mind, will, emotions) and his *body* (five senses). His life became governed by his external environment as his five senses controlled his existence.

Immediately after Adam and Eve disobeyed God's command, "*the eyes of both of them were opened, and they knew that they were naked*" (Genesis 3:7 NKJV). The word *knew* comes from the concept *to know,* from which we get our word *knowledge.* In essence, Adam and Eve suddenly became aware of their external environment. They began to live life from the knowledge they gained from their *senses.* That was the birth of *education.*

From that day on, man measured his life, worth and value by his environment. And the relationship between man and his environment gave birth to humanistic philosophy. In reality, the body and its sensual capacity became man's measure of reality. Man started living and interpreting his existence according to the *information* he gained through the senses of *his* body, instead of the *revelation* received through his spirit from the Spirit of God. Man's fall placed his body in a position it had not been designed to occupy. This change has caused man to limit his potential ability to the capabilities of his senses and his physical body.

Dignified Dirt

But we have this treasure in earthen vessels that the excellence of the power may be of God and not of us.
—2 Corinthians 4:7 NKJV

The human body was specifically designed to relate to and pick up the earth or physical realm. God did not intend the body to relate to the spiritual or supernatural world. It is essential, then, that we do not judge our true potential by the abilities or limitations of our physical bodies. For this reason, our five senses are specifically designed to "pick up" our natural environment. Our powers of sight, touch, hearing, smell, and taste are all related to the natural, physical world. The potential of our bodies is therefore governed by its physical capabilities. God never intended man to be controlled or limited by his physical body. You were not created to be intimidated by your environment.

No matter how majestic and wonderful the human body is, we must be careful to remember the reality of its composition. According to Genesis 2:7, the Manufacturer of this magnificent masterpiece made and formed it from the "*dust of the ground*." The body is 100 percent *dirt*. The apostle Paul called the body a "[heavenly] *treasure in earthen vessels*" (2 Corinthians 4:7). The principle we discussed earlier—the potential of a thing is related to its source—must be considered. If the physical body is related to the earth, it must be sustained and maintained by the earth. The body must feed on soil (dirt) in order to live (plants, animals, fish, etc.).

We must, therefore, understand that our bodies—though they have tremendous potentials, powers, capabilities and values—must never become the full measure of our potential.

What's Really Important?

But seek first His kingdom and His righteousness,
and all these things will be given to you as well.
—Matthew 6:33

I have met so many people who have everything except the knowledge of who they are. Jesus said, "Why worry about these things? Life is so much more than these things about which you worry. Life is peace and love and joy and patience and gentleness...."

Seek first the things of God and everything else you need will just fall into place. The mind controlled by the Spirit of God is full of life and peace. Peace is so important to a fulfilled life. It goes hand in hand with the life Jesus came to bring. You don't have to worry when you know what is coming. When you live by the Spirit in the realm of the unseen and the invisible, there is no reason to worry. God is holding what is in store for you, because all things that are, were and are in God.

If you'll let Him, God will work it all out for you. Through your spirit talking with His Spirit, He'll assure you everything is going to be OK. You don't have to worry if God's already told you how a particular situation is going to turn out. Relax and commit yourself to maximize your potential. Preoccupy yourself with this assignment and purpose for your life, knowing that whatever God asks for He provides for.

When we are distracted by our drive for personal security and our search for identity, we rarely achieve our true potential. We are so caught up trying to make it *through* life that we don't have time to be *in* life.

You came out of God. He created you to look and think and act like Him so you would display His greatness, majesty and sovereignty. The summit of God's desires for your life is that you will show through your being who He is.

Your potential is not determined by what you look like or how far you went in school. Nor is it determined by what others think and expect from you. God, your Creator, determines the extent of your ability. Through the Holy Spirit, He enables you to develop and experience your entire potential. God makes it possible for you to do and be much more than anyone (including you) expects. You may not look smart, but if the One who made you demands smartness from you, it's in there somewhere.

WISHING IS NOT ENOUGH—DARE TO DESIRE

Therefore I say unto you, What things soever ye desire, when ye pray, believe that ye receive them, and ye shall have them.
—MARK 11:24 KJV

Faith is not geared to what does not exist—it relates to everything that is not seen. Faith is "*being sure of what we hope for and certain of what we do not see*" (Hebrews 11:1). It deals with potential—what you yet can see, do, be and experience. Faith says, "I can't see it, but I believe it is there." Faith never deals with what you have done, but with what you yet could do.

Living by faith requires looking at the unseen, because everything that is, was in God; and *everything you could be is in you now, waiting for you to make demands on it by faith in God.*

Read Mark 11:24 above. Very often the Church has misread the word *desire.* We have expected, perhaps, that the word *desire* means "what we are dreaming about." No. *Desire* is "craving enough to sacrifice for." Only if we are willing to die for what we desire will we receive it.

God is pregnant with everything that isn't yet visible—including what you ask for in prayer. When you ask for something in faith, it is already on the way. You can't see it, but if you believe, it is already in process.

Thus, whatever you *desire* when you pray, you shall have—*but only what you desire.* Not what you *pray* for—only what you *desire when you pray.*

You must have a goal that you desire so strongly you will go after it no matter what the expense. If you are not willing to do that, you have lost already, because it is your desire for the thing that will keep you on the road of consistency. Potential needs desire to place demands upon it.

This life is full of advertisements for your attention. They come from all sides, trying to shake you from your goal. If you don't have a goal, they will provide one for you. You must know where you want to go and what you want to become. Potential needs purpose to give it direction.

When you pray, desire what you ask for. Refuse to be distracted or interrupted. The power of your potential will be revealed as you sacrifice everything to attain what you desired in prayer.

DREAMLESS POVERTY

But I have raised you up for this very purpose,
that I might show you my power and that my
name might be proclaimed in all the earth.
—EXODUS 9:16

The poorest person in the world is the person without a dream. The most frustrated person in the world is the person with a dream that never becomes reality. I am certain that every individual on this planet—no matter which race, culture, nationality or socio-economic status—has had a dream of some sort. The ability of children to dream is a natural instinct instilled by the Creator. No matter how poor or rich we are, whether we were born in the bush village of an underdeveloped nation or amid the marble floors of the aristocracy of society, we all have childhood dreams. These dreams are visual manifestations of our purpose, seeds of destiny planted in the soil of our imagination. I am convinced that God created and gave us the gift of imagination to provide us with a glimpse of our purpose in life and to activate the hidden ability within each of us. Purpose is the reason why something was made. It is the end for which the means exists. It is the source of the dream and the vision you carried in your heart from childhood. It is the key to your fulfillment.

In Exodus 9, we see Pharaoh, one of earth's most powerful rulers, was in spiritual poverty because he lacked God's dream. Yet, even Pharaoh was raised up for God's purposes. How much more are we a part of God's plan and Kingdom purpose? We just need to dream a little.

YOUR SOURCE/CREATOR DETERMINES WHAT YOU CAN DO

Jesus gave them this answer: "I tell you the truth, the Son can do nothing by himself; he can do only what he sees his Father doing, because whatever the Father does the Son also does."
—JOHN 5:19

What you can do is related to where you came from. God is serious when He says, "Without Me you can do nothing." It's not a matter of being spiritual, it just plain business sense. He created and made you. You came from Him. Therefore, the quality of your abilities is defined by God's abilities. If you want to know what you can do, find out what God can do.

God, who is omnipotent, created you to share His potential. When He took you out of Himself, He automatically gave you the ability to be creative and imaginative. You share God's potential to plan, design, and bring dreams into reality. God is full of more projects, ambitions, and proposals than you can imagine. He's the God of the impossible. But He has tied the revelation of His potential to your dreams, aspirations, and prayers. That's why God is constantly challenging you to ask Him for the impossible. The possible is no fun for God. He's already done that. It's the ideas, plans, and objectives the world hasn't seen yet that God wants to do.

You are the key to God's creative expression. You can do anything God demands of you because your Creator will never demand more of you than He's already built into you. God's saying to *you*, "Go ahead. Imagine anything you want. There's nothing you can imagine that I don't already have. I need your imagination to demand it. Your potential is related to My potential, and I am omnipotent."

God designed you to operate like He does. Faith is going into the realm where you demand out of God what's in Him that no one has seen yet. Are you in a situation that completely baffles you so that you don't know where to turn? You are the perfect candidate through which God can reveal His glory.

God gets the glory when you make demands on Him. If you want to glorify God, make Him do things He hasn't done yet. Go out on a limb and stretch your faith. That's how He created you to function. Without faith you cannot please God (see Hebrews 11:6). He demands you to perform the way He does, and He operates by faith.

God's Word on Your Potential

So don't be afraid; you are worth more than many sparrows.
—Matthew 10:31

Do you understand how much you are worth? You are equal to the value of your Source. You are as valuable as the God you came from! Stop feeling bad about other people's estimations of your value. You are special. You are worth feeling good about. God's word on your potential is the only evaluation that counts. You are not what your teacher or your spouse or your children or your boss say about you. *You are as valuable and capable as God says you are.* If you are going to release your full potential, you must understand and accept the value God places upon you and the confidence He has in your abilities.

Even as God is the One who set your value, so too He is the only One who is qualified to determine the extent of your potential. The possibilities that lie within you are dependent upon God, because the potential of a thing is always determined by the source from which it came. Even as the potential of a wooden table is determined by the strength of the tree from which it was made, so your potential is determined by God, because you came out of God. God's Word contains numerous statements that clearly define His evaluation of your potential.

YOUR POTENTIAL IS DEPENDENT UPON GOD

The grace of our Lord was poured out on me abundantly, along with the faith and love that are in Christ Jesus.

—1 Timothy 1:14

What does it mean when Jesus told His disciples that they would do greater works than He had done? Some people believe that God is afraid we're going to take His job. When we start talking about what we're going to do for God or what we're going to dream, some people say, "You'd better not think bigger than God." Well, you can never be bigger than your Source. *You can't think or plan or imagine something greater than God, because God is the source of your imagination.* He leaked part of His potential into you when He pulled you out of Himself. It's like owning a Sony video cassette recorder with multiple features. It cannot fulfill its purpose or potential until it is plugged into an electrical source. So it is for every man. We must plug into our Source.

It is imperative, then, that you understand the characteristics and qualities of God, as well as the provisions He has made to enable you to fulfill the purpose for which He created you. *Your ability to release your potential is directly related to your knowledge of God and your willingness to stay within the parameters He has established for your relationship with Him.*

YOU MUST UNDERSTAND GOD'S POTENTIAL

...so that your faith might not rest on men's wisdom, but on God's power.
—1 CORINTHIANS 2:5

Daniel 11:32 promises that "*the people that know their God shall be strong, and do exploits*" (KJV). This is true because your potential is related to God's potential, and God is *omnipotent.* The combination of *omni* (meaning "always or all full of") and *potent* (meaning "power on reserve"—from which we get the word *potential*) declares that God is always full of power. Or to say it another way, all potential is in God. Thus, people who understand that God contains all the things that He's asking them to do are not afraid to do big things. It's not *what* you know but *who* you know that enables you to do great things with God.

God is God whether you choose to use His potential or not. Your decision to live with Him or without Him does not affect who He is or what He can do. He is not diminished when you choose to replace Him with other sources. God still has the stuff you need to fulfill your potential.

When you combine the knowledge of God's omnipotence with the knowledge of who you are in God, you can resist all things that seek to overcome you and to wipe out your potential. You can be strong and do great exploits. God is the Source of your potential.

He waits to draw from His vast store to enable you to accomplish all that He demands of you.

FOCUS ON THE CREATOR

LOOK AT THE INVENTOR, NOT THE INVENTION

For although they knew God, they neither glorified Him as God nor gave thanks to Him, but their thinking became futile and their foolish hearts were darkened.
—ROMANS 1:21

Never use the creation to find out who you are, because the purpose of something is only in the mind of the One who made it. That is one of the reasons why God has a tremendous problem with idol worship. How can you identify your ability by worshiping a snake? How can you find out your worth by believing that you will come back as a rat or a roach? How dare you believe that your purpose for existence can be discovered in a relationship with a wooden statue? You will never know yourself by relating to the creation, only to the Creator. *The key to understanding life is in the source of life, not in the life itself.*

Many of the inventions man has produced would be misunderstood if only the invention were considered and not the intention of the inventor. In other words, the man who created the refrigerator had in his mind what it was supposed to be used for. He did not intend that it should be used for a trap in the backyard for a kid to be locked in and die from suffocation. Even though thousands of children have died in refrigerators, that was not the inventor's intention.

The automobile is tearing out lampposts all over the world and destroying people's homes and lives. But Mr. Ford, who first developed the assembly line to mass produce the automobile, never thought about it that way. He was thinking about transporting people and helping the human race to become a mobile community. He started us to thinking about trolleys and trains and buses. The many people who died through accidents and derailments were not part of his intention. They were not in his mind when he designed his famous Ford Model T automobile.

You Have Part of God

And just as we have borne the likeness of the earthly man,
so shall we bear the likeness of the Man from Heaven.
—1 Corinthians 15:49

You will never discover who you were meant to be if you use another person to find yourself. You will never know what you can do by using what I've done to measure your ability. You will never know why you exist if you use my existence to measure it. All you will see is what I've done or who I am. If you want to know who you are, look at God. The key to understanding life is in the source of life, not in the life itself. You are who you are because God took you out of Himself. If you want to know who you are, you must look at the Creator, not the creation.

There are three words we use to describe God. First, God is omniscient—which means He is all knowing. Second, God is omnipresent—which means God is present everywhere. Third, God is omnipotent—which means God is always potent. God is always full of power—He has in Him the potential for everything. From the beginning, God gave that same ability to be potent to all His creation. He planted within each person or thing He created—including you—the ability to be much more than it is at any one moment. Thus God created you to be omni-potent.

That is not to say we are equal to God. No. What I am saying is that the word *omnipotent* relates not only to God, but to us as well. We are always full of potential. Our potential is the dormant ability, reserved power, untapped strength and unused success God designed into each of us. What I see when I look at you is not all you are. It is only what you have become so far. Your potential is much greater than what you are right now. What you will become is much more than we could ever believe now. You are somebody because you came out of God, and He leaked some of Himself into you.

WHAT OTHERS LOOK AT IS NOT IMPORTANT

"For I know the plans I have for you," declares the Lord, "plans to prosper you and not to harm you, plans to give you hope and a future."
—JEREMIAH 29:11

Too often we believe the lies we are told. We believe that we are "no good" and worthless. Jesus says, "Not so. I came to show you that you are more than you think you are." You are the image of God.

God saw in Peter something that Peter had never seen in himself. Peter was so busy agreeing with what others called him that he missed his true potential. When we start believing what others call us, we are in big trouble. Then we throw our hands up in despair and refuse to try. People call us lazy, so we become lazy. People call us careless or stupid or clumsy, so we become careless or stupid or clumsy. Watch it! What others look at is not important. Who we are depends on what we see.

Do you believe you could walk into a prison and meet some of the greatest men and women in the world? Can you think that way? They made a mistake. They made a misjudgment. They made poor decisions. But that doesn't invalidate their potential. It doesn't destroy who they can be. In that jail there may be a murderer on death row. But when God looks at that person, He doesn't see a murderer; He sees an author or a leader or a great world changer.

Many times God is in disagreement with the people closest to you. He may even be in disagreement with you, because the only person God agrees with is Himself—only He knows your true potential. Have you failed? Go to God. He'll call you "success" and keep calling you "success" until you feel it. That's what Jesus did for Peter.

CHRIST IS IN YOU

To them God has chosen to make known among the Gentiles the glorious riches of this mystery, which is Christ in you, the hope of glory.
—COLOSSIANS 1:27

I wonder what God sees when He looks at you. I believe He sees Christ. When God looks at you, He does not see you. He sees Christ. Paul, when writing to the Colossian church, proclaimed that God had chosen to make known a mystery.

The mystery is *that Christ is in you.* That is your hope of glory. This suggests, then, that our task is not to get Christ *into* us, but *out* of us. Please get this into your minds. *What God sees when He looks at you is Christ.*

Most of us want to be like Jesus. That's not what God wants. God wants us to be like Christ. Jesus came to show us what Christ looks like when He takes on human form. But it is Christ that God's looking at. God sees Christ in you. That's the hope of glory—*Christ in you.* Let me explain.

Christ is the image of God. The word *image* does not mean "a statue of something." It means "the essence of the being." Christ is the image of God. That means when God created you, He created you in His image, and His image is Christ. That's why the Bible never calls us the Body of Jesus. Jesus was the human manifestation of the heavenly Christ. We humans on earth, with all our fallibilities and weaknesses—God pronounces on us: "You are the Body of Christ."

In other words, Christ is in us somewhere. Christ is in me. Christ is in you. God knows He is there. His image is there. So God called us Christ.

GOD'S GOT IT ALL

Those who live according to the sinful nature have their minds set on what that nature desires; but those who live in accordance with the Spirit have their minds set on what the Spirit desires.

—ROMANS 8:5

You'll never be fulfilled without God, because you are looking for what God has.

For this reason, God gives you the Holy Spirit. The only way to get out of God and into you the deep things God knows about you is through His Spirit communing with yours. The Holy Spirit searches the deep things of God—the deep things about you that you lack. God prepared and predestined those things for you before you were created. He had them in Himself and gave them to you at birth. But you don't know those things exist, because sin has capped the well and blocked the way. Only God, through the Holy Spirit, can reveal them again.

Your potential is buried in God. We think going to the moon is great—we should see what God had planned that we didn't follow. Our eyes will never see the stuff God prepared for us, nor will our ears hear it. Only the Holy Spirit can reveal to us the deep things of God that tell us who we are.

Through the gift of the Holy Spirit, you can reestablish your relationship with God. The Holy Spirit, connected with your spirit, unravels the knots that have bound your thoughts, removes the streaks that have blurred your vision and clears the debris that has hidden your potential. Working like a sculptor, He brings out the beauty hidden deep within your being, because that is the real you.

Allow God to reveal His secret wisdom concerning you. See with your eyes and hear with your ears things you have never seen or heard before. Conceive with your mind thoughts that never before have occurred to you. Cooperate with the Holy Spirit as He sucks out of God and into you the depths of the riches that God prepared for you. Live the rest of your life building an atmosphere where it is possible for the Holy Spirit to use you as He takes His bucket of hope, dips it deep into the wells of your potential and pulls it to the top of your senses. Drink deeply, growing in the knowledge of who you really are in God. That's my dream.

GOD'S "MONEY-BACK" GUARANTEE

But the Scripture declares that the whole world is a prisoner of sin, so that what was promised, being given through faith in Jesus Christ, might be given to those who believe.
—GALATIANS 3:22

The potential of a thing is determined by the demands placed upon it by the creator. This is the most amazing thing I have ever discovered about potential. The potential of a thing is determined by the demands made on it by the one who made it. A creator will not call forth from his creation something he did not put into it.

Whenever God demands something of you, don't ask whether you can do it. When you pick up the Bible and read that you can do anything if you believe, don't argue that you can't. God believes (in fact He knows) that whatever you believe hard enough, strong enough, and committed enough can come out of you because He put it in you. Your potential, like that of any other creation, is determined by the demands of your Creator.

God also graciously offers you a "Money-Back Guarantee." When you buy an appliance, a manual usually comes with it that says: "Read this before you hook it up." It also says: "You've just purchased a television that can do XYZ." You've never seen the television do that before, but the manual says it can and will because the manufacturer made it possible for it to do it. At the end of the manual, there is usually a little phrase that says: "If there is any defect, return the merchandise to the manufacturer for a free replacement." The manufacturer is guaranteeing the potential of the thing.

God mercifully says to you, "If there are any defects, return to the Manufacturer." Isn't that a blessing? If you aren't working out, take your stuff back to the Chief. The Chief will work it out. "Come unto Me," God says. "I'm the only one who can fix you." God already has guaranteed what you can do.

GOD WANTS YOU TO KNOW HIS THOUGHTS

Do not conform any longer to the pattern of this world, but be transformed by the renewing of your mind. Then you will be able to test and approve what God's will is—His good, pleasing and perfect will.
—ROMANS 12:2

When God told His people: "*For My thoughts are not your thoughts, neither are your ways My ways*" (Isa. 55:8), He was not saying He doesn't want our ways and thoughts to be like His. God was telling us: "Your thoughts and ways are not like Mine, but I'm trying to get them like Mine." God wants us to have a mind like His. He told us through the apostle Paul to be transformed by the renewing of our minds. He wants you to know and obey His will—doing what is pleasing and acceptable in His sight (see Romans 12:2). Go back to the old mind in the Garden. That's the way to think.

What a blessing it is to know that you can wake up tomorrow morning and have God's thoughts. But too often you wake up and say: "Oh, God. It's Monday."

God says: "You're not thinking like Me. This is a day I made just for you. Come on, let's go out there and give 'em Heaven." Give 'em Heaven? Yeah, that's right. There's a world out there that is hurting. Let's go give them Heaven.

But we have the attitude: "Oh God. I can never be like You."

God comes to us and says, "My child, that's exactly what I want you to do. Have the mind of Christ. Think like Me." God wants you to adopt His mind and attitude toward yourself. He desires that you think about yourself the way He does. Believe His assessment of your potential.

DON'T LET THE WORLD DETERMINE YOUR POTENTIAL

What is man that you are mindful of him,
the son of man that you care for him?
—PSALM 8:4

We have allowed the world around us to determine our potential. Teachers say to students: "You are a C student." The student then goes around believing that, and he becomes an average student for the rest of his life—an average person even. He becomes an average husband. She becomes an average wife. We become average parents and average children with average attitudes and IQs. And when we turn out to be average, our parents say: "Well, honey, you have my genes." No. They received your attitude that was transmitted to you from that teacher.

You need to shake off what people call IQs. Do you know what "IQ" means? It means Intelligence Quotient—it's what people believe your degree of intelligence is based upon some tests you take. These tests measure your motor skills, your thinking ability, your cognitive ability, your reading ability, your math ability, etc. Then based on these tests they say, "You are a D student. You are a D person." You haven't even grown up yet and they are telling you what you are going to be and do! They don't know what you are going to do.

Unfortunately, people believe what they are told based on those tests. There are thousands of examples in history of men and women who were put off and cast out as misfits. Later they turned out to be some of the world's greatest leaders. We must be careful when we start putting Intelligence Quotients on people. Your potential has nothing to do with those tests. Only God determines your potential. Your IQ is spelled *H-O-L-Y S-P-I-R-I-T.* Your IQ is something that goes far beyond the pages of a test. It goes all the way to God.

Prerequisite for Potential

Remain in Me, and I will remain in you. No branch can bear fruit by itself; it must remain in the vine. Neither can you bear fruit unless you remain in Me.
—John 15:4

Living a victorious life does not depend on us. It depends on who we are hooked up to. There are many individuals who I expected to be successful in life—their lives showed tremendous potential—but they lost their relationship with their Source. Jesus says, "If you abide in Me, you will be fruitful. But you cannot do it on your own." No branch can live by itself; it must remain attached to the vine. Neither can it bear fruit apart from the vine. Jesus is the true vine. You are a branch. If you remain in Christ and Christ in you, you will bear abundant fruit. If you do not remain in Christ, you are like a branch that withers and is thrown away. No branch can bear fruit if it is not attached. It starts going in the opposite direction. No matter how talented or gifted you are, you will never be truly fulfilled and successful apart from a personal relationship with your Creator-Source.

Thus the secret to a happy, productive life is remaining attached to your Divine Source. If you abide in Christ, His Word will abide in you. You can ask whatever you wish and it will be given to you. God will provide from the depths of His grace…freely, abundantly, victoriously. You don't have to hustle. You don't have to plead. God is always waiting to help you live a full, fruitful, complete life. From

His storehouse of riches, God will supply all you can imagine, and more because *He wants you to fulfill your potential.* So long as you remain attached to the Vine and submitted to the discipline of the Gardener, you will know God's blessings. Your potential requires a relationship with its Source.

God created you to exalt and bring glory to His name. When you bear fruit, God is glorified. His name is exalted whenever you use the abilities He stored in you. The whole purpose for your being—to reflect and increase the glory of God—is fulfilled whenever you maximize your potential. God works hard to keep us hooked up with Him. He wants His glory to fill the earth through us.

For Disciples Only

If you remain in Me and My words remain in you,
ask whatever you wish and it will be given you.
—John 15:7

Jesus' words are almost frightening—whatever you wish. God will give you whatever you ask for so long as you remain in Him. What a promise! When you open your life completely to God, the Holy Spirit's crowbar firmly resists satan's attempt to recap your well. The wealth of your potential becomes limitless and free. Whatever you imagine will be done, because God won't allow you to think it unless you can do it.

What kind of life are you living? Are you in tune with Christ or are you off doing your own thing? Is there sin clogging up your pipes, preventing you from accomplishing and achieving your maximum ability? Are you constantly hustling, struggling to make your way in the world? If you are, you probably have not become a disciple of the Risen Christ. You see, being a Christian is not enough to fulfill your potential. The word "Christian" was given to us by pagans. Jesus never called us "Christians." This term was given to the disciples in the early Church by the pagans in Antioch.

The Bible calls us "children of God" and "citizens of the Kingdom." We are God's offspring, a people who have been reconnected to their Source. Only disciples, those who are committed to abiding in Christ, will maximize their potential. A disciple is a learner who follows a teacher everywhere he goes. His goal is to learn and keep on learning until he resembles the teacher. Only a disciple experiences full potential. Because his greatest desire is to know and resemble the Master, he spends hours listening to His words. He seeks new visions, revelations and understandings concerning the Master's life and who He calls His disciples to be.

Full Potential

Then a teacher of the law came to Him and said,
"Teacher, I will follow you wherever you go."
—Matthew 8:19

Only a disciple experiences full potential. Because his greatest desire is to know and resemble the Master, he spends hours listening to His words. He seeks new visions, revelations and understandings concerning the Master's life and who He calls His disciples to be.

I do not consider myself to be great or superior to anyone else, but I decided at the age of 14 that I wanted to understand everything that God has prepared for me. I invested hours in the Word of God—large chunks…sometimes half a day. After 15 years, God said to me, "That's still not enough. Follow me." Over the years He has blessed me with a greater degree of understanding and wisdom from His Word. He's given me revelations of His life, and visions of who He is and who I am and should be. I don't want to stop. I'm not great, but I want to be one of the few. I want *you* to be one of the few. I'll lay down my life to have you be one of the few. Don't fall for the limitations of the world—the lies and deceptions of the lower nature. Find your Source and get connected. Then stay connected. God has chosen you to go and bear fruit—fruit that will last. Abide in Christ, and the Father will give you whatever you wish. Refuse to live below your privileged potential. Reach for the fruit that is still within the branches of your life. Drink deep from the vine and let your life feed others.

MAN NEEDS GOD

Jesus answered, "I am the way and the truth and the life. No one comes to the Father except through Me.
—JOHN 14:6

As the plants need dirt and the fish need water, so man needs God. If man is to realize and maximize his true potential, a relationship with God is not an option. It is a necessity. If man is to become all he was purposed to be, God is not an alternative for man, but a requirement.

This point is crucial because it helps us understand the ultimatums of Jesus and the emphatic demands of God the Father. The call of the Kingdom is not that we *should* be born of the *spirit,* but that we *must* be born of the *spirit.* Jesus didn't say, "I am *a way,*" but "*I am the way*" (John 14:6). It was also He who said, "*I am the vine; you are the branches...apart from Me you can do nothing*" (John 15:5).

This principle is also communicated in God's command to Adam in Genesis 2:17 when He stated: "*You must not eat from the tree of the knowledge of good and evil, for when you eat of it you will surely die.*" God really meant: "The day you rebel or detach yourself from your Source, you will cancel your full potential. You will never fulfill the purpose for which I created you." Sin, therefore, can be understood as man's declaration of independence from his Source. Please note that even as trees gradually die after having their roots separated from the soil, so Adam, after disobeying his Source, died spiritually. Though Adam's spiritual death was instant, the physical effects of that death were not manifested until 930 years later. This is evidence that no matter how far man progresses or how much he accomplishes, he can never experience his full potential without a personal relationship with God, his Source.

The key to knowing your true potential is to know your Source. You will never understand, realize or maximize your true and full potential without a relationship with your Source. A man without a relationship with God (his Source) has limited his potential. He can never attain what he is capable of.

GOD'S INSTRUCTION MANUAL

Your word is a lamp to my feet and a light for my path.
—PSALM 119:105

If you want a piece of equipment to operate at its maximum potential, you have to follow the manufacturer's instructions. If you don't follow the instructions, you may damage the product—or at least you won't know what you can expect from it. Only if you follow the instructions can you expect the product to meet the demands specified by the manufacturer—demands that equal what the manufacturer designed and built into the product.

We are excellent, complexly designed, tremendously built, intricately put together pieces of equipment. But we don't know what we can do. We can't even imagine the full extent of our potential. Knowing this, God sent us a manual that contains a description of our parts. He said, "Now this first part is your spirit and the second part is your soul and the third part is your body. Now here is what the body is supposed to do…here is what the soul can do…here is what the spirit can do." God also tells us the potential of this equipment called human beings. In His manual, He lists all the things we are capable of doing.

When God first presented this piece of equipment called man, something went wrong. Instead of taking it back to the manufacturer to be fixed, we took it to a second-rate, second-class, unskilled technician. And look what he did. He muddled the job.

We submitted God's equipment and product to satan, who is an unauthorized dealer with no genuine parts.

But God loved us so much that, even though the warranty had run out, He decided to take back the product. Though someone else has tried to fix us and has messed us up, God is starting all over again—and He's putting in His own parts. God is rebuilding and remaking us. He knows us better than anybody else, because He is our Creator. His Word, the Bible, reveals much about His attitude toward our potential.

YOU CAN RECEIVE WHATEVER YOU ASK

As for you, the anointing you received from Him remains in you, and you do not need anyone to teach you. But as His anointing teaches you about all things and as that anointing is real, not counterfeit—just as it has taught you, remain in Him.
—1 JOHN 2:27

We are continuing to learn how to act like our Source. One principle we need to operate within is in the area of receiving.

During His time on earth, Jesus gave His disciples a blank check. He promised them that they could receive whatever they requested.

> *Therefore I tell you, whatever you ask for in prayer, believe that you have received it, and it will be yours* (Mark 11:24).

> *If you remain in Me and My words remain in you, ask whatever you wish, and it will be given you. This is to My Father's glory, that you bear much fruit, showing yourselves to be My disciples* (John 15:7-8).

Jesus cautioned His disciples that the evidence of fruit in their lives would be the indicator that they were His disciples. He also established the key to bearing fruit as their willingness to remain in touch with Him. Insofar as you remain in touch with your Creator/Source, you have the power to ask whatever you wish and to receive what you request. That's God's promise concerning your potential. He's waiting to give you whatever you request, so long as you sink your roots deep into His Word and allow His words to influence and direct your entire life.

YOU MUST KNOW THE QUALITIES AND THE NATURE OF GOD

Be imitators of God, therefore, as dearly loved children.
—EPHESIANS 5:1

Quality is the degree of excellence or the essence of standard that makes one product better than another. The quality of a product can be no better than the qualities of the product's source. You can't use rotten apples to make a delicious apple pie. The pie will reveal the decay in the apples.

The quality of a product can also be defined as the characteristic attributes or elements that determine the product's basic nature. Those qualities arise out of the basic nature of the product's source. Or to say it another way, those things that occur naturally in a product also occur naturally in that from which the product was made.

The standards of God are the standards by which your excellence is judged, because you came out of God. Likewise, the characteristics that describe God's basic nature also describe your basic nature. If you want to know what the standards for your life are, check God's standards. If you want to know what characteristics occur in you naturally, ascertain God's inherent qualities. If God acts by a certain standard or exhibits a certain quality, that standard or quality is part of your life as well.

For example, God has the quality of faithfulness. Therefore, you have the ability to be faithful. Because God is unconditional love, you have the characteristic of love somewhere under all your hatred. Because God is merciful and long-suffering, you can be merciful and long-suffering. All the essential qualities that determine who God is and how He acts also determine who you are and how you were designed to act. Your potential is wrapped up in God because His qualities establish yours. Only when you understand and accept the nature and qualities of God can you begin to understand and accept your nature and qualities.

One of the greatest indicators of your quality and standards is expressed in God's commandments. Whatever He demands of you He knows is inside you. That's why the manual says that *"His commandments are not grievous"* (1 John 5:3 KJV).

YOU MUST COOPERATE WITH THE HOLY SPIRIT

And I will ask the Father, and He will give you another Counselor to be with you forever.
—JOHN 14:16

God's potential is far greater than anything we can ask Him to do. Everything that is visible came out of God. Everything that we yet will see is still within Him. Because we came out of God, that same potential is available to us. But there's a catch. God's power must be at work within us before we can tap that power.

> *Now to Him who is able to do immeasurably more than all we ask or imagine, according to His power that is at work within us, to Him be glory in the Church and in Christ Jesus throughout all generations, for ever and ever! Amen* (Ephesians 3:20-21).

When Jesus told His disciples that He was going away, He promised them that the Holy Spirit would come to be with them forever (see John 14:16). Moments before His ascension to Heaven, Jesus also promised that the *power of the Holy Spirit* (see Acts 1:8) would equip His followers to be His messengers.

Is the Holy Spirit present in your life? Are you flowing in a consistent, empowering relationship that undergirds your every thought, dream, and plan? Or are you trying to do great things without the power of the Spirit?

We may see a skyscraper or a space shuttle or a fancy computer and say, "That's something else. Man is really working here." But the Spirit says, "That's nothing compared to what man could do. That's what man is doing without Me. I want you to do something people cannot do unless they have Me. I want you to build people. I have the stuff to empower you to help people build new foundations and open new windows through which to see life. I want to give you a view from the top of life so you can see the way God sees." Wow! What power! That's the power that must be working inside you if you are going to do great things for God.

Your cooperation with the work of the Holy Spirit is the means by which God reveals the stuff He took from Himself and gave to you. When you are in tune with the Holy Spirit, you can do things this world has never seen. The power's there. It's up to you whether you make the connection that releases the power. If that power isn't working in you, your potential is being wasted.

YOU MUST USE CHRIST'S STRENGTH

You, dear children, are from God and have overcome them, because the One who is in you is greater than the one who is in the world.
—1 JOHN 4:4

In Philippians 4:13 Paul says, I can do everything through Him who gives me strength.

You cannot do *all things*. You can only do *all things* through *Christ*, who gives you the ability. Even though you may shout to everybody, "I can do all things," God is asking you, "Are you with Christ?" Because if you're not, your plans, dreams, and imaginations will amount to nothing. Without Christ your efforts are futile and the result is frustration.

Romans 8:31 gives me great encouragement: "*If God is for us, who can be against us?*" Now the word *for* is really the Greek word *with*. So let's put it this way: "If God is with me, who can be against me?" The implication is that if God has given you something to do and He is with you, nothing or no one is going to stop you from accomplishing what God wants you to do. I don't care who the person is or how much influence he has, if God is with you, it's not important who is coming against you.

If you are going to release your potential, you must live each day checking out who's *with* you instead of who's against you. You may be experiencing political victimization, pressure from your boss or your spouse or your parents, or unfair treatment from your family or your employer, but these influences are not the most important factors in your life. You can spend the rest of your life fighting the many people and circumstances that come against you, or you can focus on God's presence and treat them as a temporary inconvenience. If God is with you, those who accuse or harass you have no power over you.

This week can be a good one because your protection relies not on how much power your accusers have but on how much power Christ has. Jesus promises you peace and victory if you rely on His strength:

> *In this world you will have trouble. But take heart! I have overcome the world* (John 16:33).

What's the State of Your Environment?

These commandments that I give you today are to be upon your hearts. Impress them on your children. Talk about them when you sit at home and when you walk along the road, when you lie down and when you get up. Tie them as symbols on your hands and bind them on your foreheads. Write them on the doorframes of your houses and on your gates.
—Deuteronomy 6:6-9

Take a few moments to examine your environment. Is it uplifting or degrading? Does it enrich your spiritual life or detract from the work of God's Spirit in your heart? Is obedience to God the norm for those with whom you spend your days or do rebellion and disobedience characterize the lifestyles of your closest friends?

Moses instructed the Israelites to immerse themselves in God's commandments in Deuteronomy 6:6-9 (see above).

I recommend the same practice to you. For out of a heart centered on God flow His gifts of faith, forgiveness, and obedience. These essential ingredients of your God-designed environment testify to a relationship with the Risen Christ that clings to the promise of His presence and delights in the joy of His fellowship. They are the heritage of those who maintain a positive environment so their potential can be released, because a relationship with God always provides the right environment.

A Checklist for Your Environmental Conditions

1. Who are your friends?
2. What books do you read?
3. What movies do you watch?
4. What magazines fill your shelves?
5. What are your hobbies?
6. What are your recreational activities?
7. Who feeds your musical appetites?
8. Who are your heroes?
9. Who feeds you spiritually?
10. Are the conditions of your home, school, work, or play conducive to your goals in life?

All the above should be carefully screened, analyzed, and adjusted to feed, activate, enhance, and foster the release of your potential.

TURNING POTENTIAL INTO ACTION

FROM THOUGHT TO ACTION

He replied, "...I tell you the truth, if you have faith as small as a mustard seed, you can say to this mountain, 'Move from here to there' and it will move. Nothing will be impossible for you."
—MATTHEW 17:20

A *thought* is a silent word, so a word is an exposed thought. Everything in life starts in the thought form—it's a thought first. After it's said, it is no longer a thought. It becomes a word.

The next step is an *idea*. An idea is the concept of the thought—it has moved into a reality. Ideas are potentials.

The third level of operation is what I call *imagination*. Imagination changes an idea into a plan. If you have an idea it can come and go. You have many ideas in a day—what to cook, what to wear, what to do. You may decide the night before what you are going to wear in the morning and then wake up with a different idea. Ideas change. But if an idea develops into an imagination, it means the idea has become a plan. It is still not written or drawn, but it is in your head. Imagination is therefore a plan that is not documented. It is a visual display of your thoughts and ideas. Ephesians 3:20 challenges us to believe God is able and willing to do "*exceeding abundantly above all that we ask or think*" (NKJV). He dares us to use our imaginations.

If you want to be successful in life, take your ideas and turn them into imagination; then take imagination and duplicate it physically. Put it down. Let it become a plan of action.

Many people never get beyond the idea stage. That's sad. They are usually followers. The people who get to the imagination stage often talk a lot but they do nothing. They are dreamers. But when a man or woman takes his imagination and puts it on paper, you are looking at a visionary who is becoming a missionary. Visionaries see great things in their minds. Many visionaries are in the graveyard. They had visions, but their visions never made it to mission. When a visionary becomes a missionary, you have a man or woman who is going to change the world.

FREED TO OBEY

And this is love: that we walk in obedience to His commands. As you have heard from the beginning, His command is that you walk in love.
—2 JOHN 1:6

When God placed Adam and Eve in the garden of Eden, He said, "*You are free to eat from any tree in the garden; but you must not eat from the tree of the knowledge of good and evil, for when you eat of it you will surely die*" (Genesis 2:16-17). God gives you freedom, but He also puts some limitations on you. Whenever you violate your limitations, you are in rebellion against God. The only limitations of your potential are violations of God's Word. If you do anything that doesn't violate the Word of God, you are within your freedom. God gives you freedom to do anything except disobey Him. That's a tremendous freedom. You are free to do anything within the context of God's Word. If God says it's cool, go for it, because the possibilities of your life are all connected with God.

God comes into your life with pruning shearers to free you from your disobedience and rebellion. He comes to take out those things that are stopping you from developing and growing and obeying. Anything that is contrary to the Word of God is subject to God's pruning. He comes into your life to help you clean up your act. He wants you to enjoy the freedom of obedience and life within His limitations. Bearing a pruning shear, God trims the useless and dead wood from your life so you can draw from Him the fresh fullness of your potential. You are cleansed through the word Jesus speaks to you when you asked Him to forgive you. The lid on your well, put there through your disobedience and satan's deception, has been pried off. You are clean and free to do *anything* that doesn't violate God's Word—free to be all you were created to be and do (whatever He says you can do). What freedom!—freedom that can last, so long as you remain hooked up to God. The Son is Life and the Father is the Maximizer.

YOUR SOURCE/CREATOR DETERMINES THE CONDITIONS YOU NEED FOR OPTIMUM PERFORMANCE

The Lord brought me forth as the first of His works, before His deeds of old; I was appointed from eternity, from the beginning, before the world began.
—PROVERBS 8:22-23

Your Creator/Source is the only One who is qualified to define your optimal environment. He does so through His laws and commandments. God's laws establish the elements of your ideal environment and set the necessary requirements for consistent, healthy growth. *God's commandments help you to maintain your environment.* They serve as indicators of the state of your health and the condition of your environment. Your well-being is dependent upon your understanding of God's laws and your obedience to His commandments. You can't afford to break God's commandments because disobedience brings a polluted environment, which stunts and impedes the release of your potential.

You have the potential to perform great exploits for God. But if you fail to maintain the environment God decrees, nothing will happen in your life. It doesn't matter how much you brag about what you can do or what you would like to do, or how much you can see and dream and imagine; if God's requirements aren't met, you aren't going to expose your true self!

God not only wants to share with you His plans for your life, He also wants you to understand the variety of experiences that He deems necessary for you to effectively fulfill those plans. Many people try one thing after another as they search for the meaning of their lives. They move from one job to the next, from one church to the next, from one town to the next, and from one spouse to the next. When the going gets a little rough, they move on to something else. They never hang in there long enough to make any progress.

Jesus tells a story about a woman who swept her house and searched carefully until she found the coin she had lost (see Luke 15:8-10). She didn't just sit in her chair and mourn her loss; she got up and worked until she found it. She translated her desire into a plan, and her plan into *action.* The release of your potential requires that you stick with something until you see it through. It's not enough just to *think* about what God wants from your life; you have to get up and do it.

Work is the method God established to release His potential. The creation story tells us that God worked so hard creating the world that He was tired when He finished. Because you came out of God, work is also required of you to bring forth all the invisible jewels that lay hidden inside you. God established work as a priority that brings fulfillment and contentment. *He designed you to work out your potential.*

YOUR SOURCE/CREATOR DETERMINES WHY YOU EXIST

To one he gave five talents of money, to another two talents, and to another one talent, each according to his ability.
—MATTHEW 25:15

You will never know your purpose unless you figure out why God created you. Only God knows your purpose, because He determined it when He gave you life.

The direction you need to live a satisfying and rewarding life cannot be found in your family, your teachers, your employer, your pastor, or your coworkers. They are creatures even as you are. *The only way you can discover your purpose is through a relationship with the One who made you.* God's original desires for you shape your potential because He designed you with care to meet the demands He wants to make on you. The release of your total potential requires that you continually seek God as you try to understand what He had in mind when He laid out His plans for your life.

Jesus tells the story of a man who was going on a journey. Before he left home, the master called his servants to him and gave each of them a portion of his resources. When he returned, he asked each servant to give an accounting of what they had received. Although the master didn't expect each servant to have equal resources when he returned, he did expect that they would have used and increased the property he had entrusted to them (see Matthew 25:14-30).

God has determined the resources you need to live a happy, productive life, because He is the only One who knows what you need to meet the demands He will place upon you. If you are constantly comparing your resources with those of other people, you will be blinded both to the richness of what God has entrusted to you and the tasks He wants you to accomplish using what you have. The release of your full potential demands that you examine your life carefully so you can identify both the many assets God has given you and the purpose for which He gave them. God will not entrust you with more resources until you use wisely what He's already given you.

YOU CAN ACCOMPLISH IMPOSSIBILITIES

Everything is possible for him who believes.
—MARK 9:23

The basic principles that apply to the potential of all things also apply to your potential. God, your Source/Creator, is the Definer of your potential. The Bible has much to say about your personal worth and your unique capabilities. You can dominate, rule and subdue the earth. You can be fruitful and multiply. You have the capacity to imagine and plan and believe anything into reality.

Consistent with man's ability to make plans and bring them to completion is his power to believe impossibilities into possibilities. Jesus said to the father of a demon-possessed boy:

> *Everything is possible for him who believes* (Mark 9:23).

This ability is an extension of man's potential to operate like God.

The Gospel of Matthew tells a story of faith in which one of Jesus' disciples, for a moment, accomplished the impossible. Peter, with the other disciples, was in a boat on the Sea of Galilee when Jesus came to them, walking on the water. The disciples, thinking it was a ghost, cried out in fear. After Jesus had identified Himself, impetuous Peter replied, "*Lord, if it's You…tell me to come to You on the water*" (Matthew 14:28).

Now you and I know that the physical laws of nature should have prevented Peter from walking to Jesus. But the laws of faith are different. When Jesus told him to come, Peter got out of the boat and went toward Jesus. Only when he became fearful of the wind and the waves did he begin to sink. "*Immediately Jesus reached out His hand and caught him. 'You of little faith,' He said, 'why did you doubt?'*" (Matthew 14:31).

If you are a man or woman of faith, you have the awesome power to operate by the laws of faith. Impossibilities become possibilities when you use this potential.

YOU CAN INFLUENCE THINGS ON EARTH AND IN HEAVEN

Then Jesus came to them and said, "All authority in Heaven and on earth has been given to Me."
—MATTHEW 28:18

Man's tremendous potential includes the capacity to influence both physical and spiritual things. This capacity is a colossal power that we seldom use. Jesus pointed to this power after Peter confessed, *"You are the Christ, the Son of the living God"* (Matthew 16:16).

> *Jesus replied, "Blessed are you, Simon son of Jonah, for this was not revealed to you by man, but by My Father in Heaven. And I tell you that you are Peter, and on this rock I will build My church, and the gates of Hades will not overcome it. I will give you the keys of the kingdom of Heaven; whatever you bind on earth will be bound in Heaven, and whatever you loose on earth will be loosed in Heaven* (Matthew 16:17-19).

Jesus is encouraging us to look beyond the physical circumstances of our lives to the spiritual dimension. If you are dealing with just the physical aspects of your life, you are missing the real thing. Look beyond the problems in your job or with your spouse or in your church to the spiritual realities that underlie them. Say in the natural what you want to happen in the spiritual. The power to affect both realms is yours. You hold the keys to your effective participation in God's Kingdom, because all authority in Heaven and on earth belongs to Jesus (see Matthew 28:18), and He has shared that power with you.

YOU MUST HAVE FAITH IN GOD

He replied, "If you have faith as small as a mustard seed, you can say to this mulberry tree, 'Be uprooted and planted in the sea,' and it will obey you."
—LUKE 17:6

If I give you a tree as a gift and I tell you it is an avocado tree, you will tell every person who asks you what kind of tree is in your front yard that it's an avocado tree. Now you haven't picked any avocados from that tree, but you still dare to say it's an avocado tree. Why? Because you have faith in me that the tree is what I say it is. You believe that somewhere in that tree there are many avocados. Faith is simply believing and acting on the words and integrity of another. Faith in God is to believe and act on what He says.

The words of Jesus as recorded in the Gospel of Mark admonish us to have faith in God.

> *"Have faith in God," Jesus answered. "I tell you the truth, if anyone says to this mountain, 'Go, throw yourself into the sea,' and does not doubt in his heart but believes that what he says will happen, it will be done for him"* (Mark 11:22-23).

What Jesus is really saying is, "Have the God kind of faith." Don't put your faith in your own faith or in the faith of other people or in the mountains or in anything that you expect to happen because of your faith. Put your faith in God, because it's your faith in Him that will accomplish the moving of mountains. You can't speak to the mountain and expect it to move unless you are connected to God. Apart from Him you don't have the power to complete such monumental tasks.

THE FAITH PROCESS

It is written: "I believed; therefore I have spoken." With that same spirit of faith we also believe and therefore speak, because we know that the one who raised the Lord Jesus from the dead will also raise us with Jesus and present us with you in His presence.
—2 CORINTHIANS 4:13-14

Faith begins with *belief.* Actually, faith in someone or something requires unquestioning belief that does not require proof or evidence from the one in whom you have faith. The New Testament word for faith, *pistos*, means "to believe another's testimony." Thus, faith requires you to function by believing first, instead of seeing or feeling first.

That often creates a problem, because faith requires putting your body under the control of your spirit. Your body says, "I'm not going to believe it until I see it." But God says, "If you're going to operate like Me, you aren't going to see it until you believe it!" One operates by sight, the other by faith.

Living by faith also requires that you put your soul under the control of your spirit. Your soul governs your emotions, your will, and your mind. When you live from your soul, you allow information from your physical body to govern your decisions.

After you believe God's promises, you must begin to see (conceive) them in your life. Seeing and looking are very different.

Looking regards the outward appearance, while seeing considers the existence of things that are not yet visible.

After you can see something, you have to *release* it. In Genesis, God looked at the darkness and saw light. Although the light existed, it was not made visible until God spoke it into being.

Faith is required of all who want to please God. Hebrews 11:6 warns us that "*without faith it is impossible to please God, because anyone who comes to Him must believe that He exists and that He rewards those who earnestly seek Him,*" and Romans 1:17 says, "*The righteous will live by faith.*" You were created to live by faith. God established faith as the only system through which men and women can touch His power. Potential demands faith, and faith makes demands on potential.

Righteousness, which, in the Bible, means "to enjoy a right relationship with God," is impossible without God's act of salvation in Jesus Christ. Jesus' death on the Cross freed you from eternal death, which is the penalty for your sin. For those who have received new life in Christ, God renders a verdict of "not guilty."

Faith Is a Requirement, Not an Option

Jesus replied, "I tell you the truth, if you have faith and do not doubt, not only can you do what was done to the fig tree, but also you can say to this mountain, 'Go, throw yourself into the sea,' and it will be done."
—Matthew 21:21

Faith is not an option for the Christian. It is a necessity. If God tells you to get moving, He doesn't want you to stand around until you see the evidence that says you should get moving. He wants you to risk, simply because He is asking you to move.

In fact, faith is not an option for human beings in general. A person who lives on anything but faith is going to live a depressing life. He will be so consumed by his environment and the circumstances of his life that he will never venture beyond the known to release the vast potential inside him. Faith is the source of hope, and no man can live without hope. Faith is the fuel of the future and the energy of anticipation.

Many people are wrecks because they try to live without faith. That's unfortunate because the Scriptures are clear that faith in God is the prerequisite for receiving what you believe, conceive, and release.

> *Therefore I tell you, whatever you ask for in prayer, believe that you have received it, and it will be yours* (Mark 11:24).

Faith is the catalyst that makes things happen. It lifts you above the outward evidence of your life and empowers you to bring light out of darkness. Remember, you will receive whatever you believe. If you expect trouble, you will get it. If you trust God and expect Him to work in the midst of your distressing circumstances, sooner or later you will see evidence of His presence.

Life without faith is foolish because life is not always what it seems. What you see or feel is not the whole story. Believe that things are going to work out. Reject the garbage that discourages you by taking your eyes off God—"You're never going to own a house. You can't even pay this rent. How're you going to afford a mortgage?"—and believe that you are going to make it. Make plans and, by faith, release your dreams by saying: "I know what I see, but I also know what I believe. I'm going to keep believing in my dreams, because all things are possible with God." Praise Him that you don't have to live by what you see. Believe in His promises and expect Him to move mountains for you.

POVERTY AND WEALTH—BIBLICAL VIEWPOINT

Do not love sleep or you will grow poor;
stay awake and you will have food to spare.
—PROVERBS 20:13

You can never change the world by being controlled by the earth. All resources should lead to God, their ultimate Source.

Most of us at some point in our lives have wished that we had more resources than we actually have. We have looked at another person's resources and envied them, bemoaning our apparent poverty. This attitude is a stumbling block to releasing our full potential because God's view of poverty and wealth is very different from ours. He is more concerned with what we *do* with what we have, than with how much we *have.*

Many people believe that God favors the rich and keeps things from the poor, but that is not what the Bible teaches. God loves and cares for all people, rich or poor:

> *The poor man and the oppressor have this in common:*
> *The Lord gives sight to the eyes of both* (Proverbs 29:13).

Therefore, it is not that God makes rich people and poor people. Rather God makes all people—some who become rich and some who become poor. The key is what you do with the resources God gives you.

> *Lazy hands make a man poor, but diligent hands bring wealth* (Proverbs 10:4).

Poverty is not a gift from God but the result of your actions. The degree of wealth or poverty in which you find yourself is to a large extent related to the way you are using what you have. A hardworking person becomes rich, while a lazy person becomes poor. Your success is not determined by what you have, but by what you do with what you have.

It doesn't matter what your family is like economically. You can decide that you aren't going to stay where your family is. You can resolve to try new things and to work hard. God wants energetic, diligent people. He's always searching for men and women who will look beyond their circumstances to their possibilities.

THE EFFECTIVE USE OF RESOURCES

...in order that satan might not outwit us.
For we are not unaware of his schemes.
—2 CORINTHIANS 2:11

One of the greatest problems facing the Church is not the lack of resources but the *lack of use* of resources. Every resource God gave to Adam is available to us. But we don't use all those resources. Instead of seeing the possibilities in everything God has given us, we categorize our resources and refuse to use some of them because we are threatened by the world's use of them.

What the world is doing or building is not the problem. Worldly people don't have any more resources than those they are currently using to solve the world's problems. This is not true for the Church. The Church is not solving the world's problems because we misunderstand the resources that are available to us.

The Bible affirms that all things were made by God, and "*without Him nothing was made that has been made*" (John 1:3). That means everything belongs to God. The Bible also affirms that "*God saw all that He had made, and it was very good*" (Genesis 1:31). That means every resource God has given man is good.

The Scriptures are clear that God is the Creator and satan is a perverter. Satan cannot create anything. He can only pervert what God created. Therein lies the source of our problem. Counterfeits abound in our world. They are the result of satan's misuse and abuse of God's resources.

God gives you resources so you can accomplish what He put you here to do. He gives them to you to live *on*, not *for*. When you start living for money you're in trouble. When your job becomes the most important thing in your life, you're in for hard times. Whenever a resource becomes more important than the purpose for which God gave it, you have crossed the line between using it and abusing it.

YOUR AVAILABLE RESOURCES—SPIRITUAL

...Man does not live on bread alone, but on every word that comes from the mouth of God.
—MATTHEW 4:4

There are five types of resources you must understand and control if you are going to become a successful person: spiritual, physical, material, the soul, and time.

SPIRITUAL RESOURCES

First, God has given you spiritual resources. Because God created you in His own image, He gave you the ability to tap into Him.

Spiritual food is available to you in a variety of forms. First and foremost, you must feed your spirit from the Word of God:

Blessed rather are those who hear the Word of God and obey it (Luke 11:28).

Stay in a good place where they teach the Word of God. Keep staying there until you get what they are feeding you. You may fall as you learn to walk according to the Spirit, but that's OK. Just pick yourself up and try again. As long as you're feeding yourself spiritual food, you're growing, changing, and getting stronger. You may not see that growth, but it's happening whether you see it or not.

> *The gifts of the Spirit are also resources to feed you: Now to each one the manifestation of the Spirit is given for the common good* (1 Corinthians 12:7).

These resources include the word of wisdom, the word of knowledge, faith, miracles, healings, tongues, interpretation of tongues and prophecy. God gave these wonderful gifts to build up the Church. If you have accepted Jesus as your Lord and Savior, they are available to you.

God also provides *His armor* to protect you (see Ephesians 6:13-18).

Truth, righteousness, peace, faith, salvation, prayer. What wealth! Add to them fasting, giving, and forgiving. If your spirit and God's Spirit are in touch, each is yours to use. They can make the difference between a good day and a bad day, between a dismal life and a successful life. Your circumstances may not change as quickly as you'd like, but I guarantee you that your attitudes will.

YOUR AVAILABLE RESOURCES—PHYSICAL AND MATERIAL

Then God said, "I give you every seed-bearing plant on the face of the whole earth and every tree that has fruit with seed in it. They will be yours for food."
—GENESIS 1:29

We will continue to study the five types of resources you must understand and control if you are going to become a successful person: spiritual, physical, material, the soul, and time.

PHYSICAL RESOURCES

God's provisions include physical resources. When God created you, He created your spirit and put it into your body. Because of God's gift of life, your wonderful, physical machine can breathe, move, eat, and heal itself. Many of the pleasures you enjoy in life are yours because God took the dust of the ground and fashioned your body. You can see the beauty of flowers, a sunset or a rainbow. You can taste the sweetness of honey or of fruit fresh from the tree. You can feel the love of your children as their little arms encircle your neck and your ears hear those sweetest of words: I love you Mommy. I love you Daddy.

As wondrous as your body is, you may not use it however you desire. Choose carefully the kind of fuel you give your body. Be aware that your body is for food, and food is for your body. Like any of God's resources, improper care and inappropriate attitudes toward your body can result in misuse and abuse:

> *"Everything is permissible for me"—but not everything is beneficial. "Everything is permissible for me"—but I will not be mastered by anything. "Food for the stomach and the stomach for food"—but God will destroy them both. The body is not meant for sexual immorality, but for the Lord, and the Lord for the body. ...Do you not know that your bodies are members of Christ Himself?* (1 Corinthians 6:12-13,15)

Material Resources

The third kind of resource God has given you is material resources. God's conversation with Adam in the Garden of Eden shows that God provided well for Adam's needs (see Genesis 1:29 above).

Genesis 1 also reveals that God also provided gold, aromatic resin, onyx, and a river for watering the earth. Indeed, the vast geological and geographical resources of this earth are all part of God's gracious provision for your life.

YOUR AVAILABLE RESOURCES—SOUL AND TIME

What good will it be for a man if he gains the whole world, yet forfeits his soul? Or what can a man give in exchange for his soul?
—MATTHEW 16:26

We are studying the five types of resources you must understand and control if you are going to become a successful person: spiritual, physical, material, the soul, and time.

THE RESOURCES OF THE SOUL

You are spirit and you have a soul. The assistance you receive from your mind, your will, and your feelings are the resources of the soul that God has given you.

Think what life would be like without these resources. They are the primary means by which you express who you are. Your spirit depends on your soul, as does your body. The Scriptures recognize the importance of the soul: "*Dear friends, I urge you, as aliens and strangers in the world, to abstain from sinful desires, which war against your soul*" (1 Peter 2:11).

Jesus came after the soul because the spirit is easy. It is through your will, your feelings, and your mind that satan seeks to attack you. If you guard your soul, your spirit and your body will be well. Their condition depends on the state of your soul. This is clearly revealed in the Bible: "*For as* [a man] *thinketh in his heart, so is he*" (Proverbs 23:7 KJV).

Belief takes place in the spirit, but thinking takes places in the soul. You can believe one thing and think something completely different. What you think is what you become, not what you believe. That's why Jesus came preaching repentance. He knew that our thoughts influence us much more than our beliefs.

The resources of your soul are not available to you unless you allow God to transform your mind.

The Resource of the Time

Time is a temporary interruption in eternity. It is a commodity that can be neither bought nor sold. The only thing you can do with time is use it. If you don't use it, you lose it. The apostle Paul encouraged members of the early Church to "[redeem] *the time* (Ephesians 5:16 KJV) or "[make] *the most of every opportunity*" (NIV).

The only time you have is now. Get busy and use it wisely. Say, "God, I am going to use every minute of my day constructively, effectively, and efficiently." Time is God's gift—one of His precious resources. Refuse to be one of those who waste time and then complain because they don't have enough time. Make the hours of your day count.

THE PRINCIPLE OF EXPERIENCE—PART 1

If we claim to have fellowship with Him yet walk in the darkness, we lie and do not live by the truth.
—1 JOHN 1:6

Experience may be defined as "the observation of facts as a source of knowledge and skill gained by contact with facts and events." By its very nature, experience is a product of the past and is, therefore, limited to and controlled by previous exposure. In spite of the fact that experience may be valuable for making decisions and judgments concerning the future, it is important to know that any significant measurement of growth, development, expansion, or advancement will require experience to submit to the substance of the unknown through faith.

Unfortunately, experience has compelled many promising people to cower in the shadows of fear and failure because they were not willing to venture out into the uncharted frontiers of new possibilities. Experience is given not to determine the limits of our lives, but to create a better life for us. Experience is a tool to be used!

My experience with driving over the years has conditioned me to drive a car monitored by the speed limits established by the society. Therefore, my driving capacity has become subject to the accepted norms of 45-60 mph. The fact that I have driven my car at 45-60 mph for over 25 years does not cancel the automobile's capacity to travel at 100-180 mph. *In essence, experience does not cancel capacity.* Therefore, my car's capacity is determined not by my use of that capacity but by the capacity built into the car by the manufacturer.

THE PRINCIPLE OF EXPERIENCE—PART 2

By faith Enoch was taken from this life, so that he did not experience death; he could not be found, because God had taken him away. For before he was taken, he was commended as one who pleased God.
—HEBREWS 11:5

Experience is given not to determine the limits of our lives, but to create a better life for us. Experience is a tool to be used!

In essence, experience does not cancel capacity. At any point in our lives, we are the sum total of all the decisions we have made, the people we have met, the exposure we have had, and the facts we have learned. In essence, every human is a walking history book. Nevertheless, we must keep in mind that our personal history is being made and recorded every day, and our past experience was once our future. Therefore, we must be careful not to allow our past to determine the quality of our future. Instead, we must use our experience to help us make better decisions, always guarding against the possibility that it may limit our decisions. *Remember, your ability is never limited to your experience.*

This world is filled with millions of individuals who are capable of traveling at a maximum capacity of 180 mph, but they have settled for 55 mph. Because they have overtaken some folks or have exceeded the expectations of a few others, they have compared their lives to these persons and have accepted mediocrity as excellence.

Determine not to let your past experience limit your capacity. Be grateful for the lessons of the past, then accelerate with confidence on to the autobahn of life, being careful to obey only those signs that have been established by your Creator, who admonishes you, "*All things are possible if you only believe*" (see Mark 9:23).

UNDER THE CIRCUMSTANCES

...equip you with everything good for doing His will, and may He work in us what is pleasing to Him, through Jesus Christ, to whom be glory for ever and ever. Amen.
—HEBREWS 13:21

One reason we fail to progress in fulfilling our purpose is that we have accepted the present state of our lives as the best we can do under the circumstances.

This concept, "under the circumstances," serves to imprison us and to immobilize our God-given ambition because too many of us have surrendered to the status quo and have become prisoners of the war for our minds. We forget that "circumstances" are simply temporary arrangements of life to which we are all exposed. We overlook or disregard the fact that these circumstances are designed to identify, expose, develop, refine, and maximize our true potential. It's not what happens to us that matters, but what we do with what happens. Much of the time we are not responsible for our circumstances, but we are always responsible for our response to those circumstances. *One key to maximizing your potential is to become dissatisfied with the circumstances that restrict, limit, and stifle your potential.*

Many people know that they possess great potential, that they have a significant purpose in life, but they still fail to move beyond good intentions to experience the fullness of their lives. Why?

Their comfort is greater than their passion. They are more concerned with fitting in than with standing out.

Remember, *you will never change anything that you are willing to tolerate.* Your Creator wants you to consciously choose to fulfill your purpose and maximize your potential because in so doing you will bring glory to His name. Unfortunately, history gives evidence of only a few rare individuals who, driven by a passion to achieve a cherished vision in their hearts, initiated their own deliverance, rose above the tide of the norm, and impacted their generation and ours.

A second significant key to maximizing potential is the unassuming benefits of "crisis." Crises, as defined by author Dick Leider, are life's "wake-up" calls. These alarms are often the catalysts that impel us to become fully conscious of our mediocre lives.

Move Beyond Your Comfort Zone

Like an eagle that stirs up its nest and hovers over its young, that spreads its wings to catch them and carries them on it pinions. The Lord alone [leads you].
—Deuteronomy 32:11-12

How many stories have you heard about individuals who, after a close call with death or disease, suddenly change their lifestyles and their attitude toward life? Often their priorities, and sometimes their entire value system, change. The biblical record bears witness to the efficacy of a crisis to get people back on track. Beginning with Abraham, and continuing on to Joseph, Moses, David, Jonah, Peter, and most significantly the apostle Paul, God used the interjection of a major crisis to lead these heroes of faith to move beyond mediocrity to life at the maximum.

Remember, *we cannot become what we were born to be by remaining what we are.* Just as the mother eagle removes the comforts of her feathery nest to "disturb" the young eaglets into flying, so our Creator moves us beyond our comfort zones so that we are forced to fly. Without this stirring, most of us would never fly.

An eagle that doesn't fly cannot fulfill its purpose. Likewise, your life will lack purpose and focus until you discover your wings. This discovery will require both wisdom and courage because the thrill of flying always begins with the fear of falling. Yet you are not left alone to find your wings because God, through the prophet Moses, promises to undertake for you.

He will give definition to the crises of your life and inspire you to move on into all He has planned for you. Indeed, the greatest gift God can offer you is to push you into a crisis of temporary discomfort that requires you to try your wings. This pushing into crisis is His supreme act of love, akin to that of a mother eagle that pushes her young from the nest to force them to fly.

LEARN TO WORK HARD

SHORTCUTS DON'T WORK

...and observe what the Lord your God requires: Walk in His ways, and keep His decrees and commands, His laws and requirements, as written in the Law of Moses, so that you may prosper in all you do and wherever you go.
—1 KINGS 2:3

Ben Johnson is an athlete from Canada who set many world records. In 1987 he set the world record in the 100-yard dash at 9.83 seconds. In 1988 he broke his own record, winning the race in 9.79. But it is difficult to be correct in calling that a world record because the last record set was not the record of Ben Johnson. It was the record of a steroid pill. That record belongs to Ben Johnson plus the chemicals.

We will never know Ben Johnson's potential as far as running the 100-yard dash is concerned. Could he have run 100 yards in 9.79 seconds without the chemical? Possibly, but we will never know because Ben Johnson negated his potential by trying a shortcut. There was no reason for his shortcut. He had a world record. He had his name in history, and it was a good name. How sad to destroy a good name by a little bit of chemical.

I picked up a magazine on an airplane in which there was an advertisement that said, "Would you like a doctorate degree? Call us." I often read that advertisement and wonder how many have called them. If I did not realize that you cannot get something for nothing, I probably would have called them. Many have. There are people out there with doctorate degrees, or with doctorate letters in front of their names, who will never know their potential. They didn't allow themselves the chance to see what they could really do. They have the degrees, but they didn't fulfill the requirements.

There are no shortcuts to developing your potential. You will never know what you might have achieved if you use a crutch to get there. You'll never know what you may have learned if you get a degree without fulfilling the requirements. You will never know what you can do if you attempt to obtain it by a shortcut. Shortcuts negate potential. They destroy the possibilities God planted within you.

What Rules Your Life?

Misfortune pursues the sinner, but prosperity is the reward of the righteous. A good man leaves an inheritance for his children's children, but a sinner's wealth is stored up for the righteous.
—Proverbs 13:21-22

Many workers see their jobs as dull, laborious, repetitious, tedious, and irritating. This attitude toward work has become of great concern to governments, corporations, and the media. As major problems with poor quality work, reduced productivity, and declining services cripple economic growth, the need and the desire to offer incentives and motivational exercises grow. Thus, aerobics classes, fitness rooms, and running tracks have become the focus of much effort and expense in the workplace.

No matter how we dissect things, the power in our society can be reduced to two basic elements: *God* and *money*. They are the major forces in our world. Jesus warned that we would serve one or the other:

> *No one can serve two masters. Either he will hate the one and love the other, or he will be devoted to the one and despise the other. You cannot serve both God and money* (Matthew 6:24).

Which one you serve has a significant impact on the release of your potential, because the basic power in your life determines what motivates you. If money motivates you, greed will control your actions. If God empowers you, His purposes for your life will control you. The Scriptures promise that God will meet the needs of those who give their first allegiance to Him:

> *Therefore I tell you, do not worry about your life, what you will eat or drink; or about your body, what you will wear. Is not life more important than food, and the body more important than clothes? ...For the pagans run after all these things, and your heavenly Father knows that you need them. But seek first His kingdom and His righteousness, and all these things will be given to you as well* (Matthew 6:256,32-33).

They also warn that allegiance to money brings trouble and financial bankruptcy: *The greedy man brings trouble to his family...* (Proverbs 15:27).

This is true because the love of money promotes corrupt morals and perverted values. The need to accumulate more and more material wealth overshadows God's concerns of truth and honesty until deception and dishonesty determine what you do and how you do it.

DO YOU WORK OR GO TO A JOB?

The wages of the righteous bring them life, but the income of the wicked brings them punishment.
—PROVERBS 10:16

The love of money promotes corrupt morals and perverted values. The need to accumulate more and more material wealth overshadows God's concerns of truth and honesty until deception and dishonesty determine what you do and how you do it.

> *The wicked man earns deceptive wages, but he who sows righteousness reaps a sure reward. ...Whoever trusts in his riches will fall, but the righteous will thrive like a green leaf* (Proverbs 11:18,28).

This conflict between God and money is very evident in our attitudes toward work.

Most of us want jobs, but we don't want to work. We want the money, but we don't want to expend the energy. Nothing is as depressing and frustrating as having someone on a job who's not interested in working. People who want a job without the work are a detriment. They are more interested in being job keepers than workers. They are more concerned with receiving a paycheck than in doing good work.

This attitude is completely contrary to God's concept of work. God wants you to be a good worker, not a good job keeper. He is more interested in your attitude toward work than the status of your checkbook. He has the power to increase your bank account balance, but He can't force you to have a positive attitude toward work.

OUR NEGATIVE VIEW OF WORK

Moreover, when God gives any man wealth and possessions, and enables him to enjoy them, to accept his lot and be happy in his work—this is a gift of God.
—ECCLESIASTES 5:19

Thomas Edison was a great inventor. Many of the things we enjoy today, including the electric light, are the fruit of his willingness to be responsible for the possibilities hidden within him. He was not afraid to roll up his sleeves and work out his potential to make visible that which existed but we couldn't see. His life mirrored his words: "Genius is 1 percent inspiration and 99 percent perspiration."

Too often we allow the pain and perspiration of work to hide its blessings. We assume that work is a necessary evil without looking for the good it brings. The source of our misconceptions lies in the fact that we equate sin and work. Although work does not exist because of sin, sin did change the conditions of work.

> *Cursed is the ground because of you; through painful toil you will eat of it all the days of your life. It will produce thorns and thistles for you, and you will eat the plants of the field. By the sweat of your brow you will eat your food until you return to the ground, since from it you were taken* (Genesis 3:17-19).

Work as God planned it was given to man before sin entered the world. The account of Adam naming the animals precedes the account of Adam and Eve's disobedience. Work as we know it—with its pain, sweat, and struggle—reveals the devastation of Adam and Eve's disobedience.

When God told Adam, "Dominate this world I made. Rule this planet," life was new and fresh, and Adam had no knowledge of the power God had built into his brain. So God required Adam to come up with a different name for every animal. As he started naming the birds of the air and the beasts of the field, Adam discovered his potential. Thus, work is a blessing that reveals what you can do. It is the master key to releasing your potential.

MISCONCEPTIONS ABOUT WORK

Six days do your work, but on the seventh day do not work, so that your ox and your donkey may rest and the slave born in your household, and the alien as well, may be refreshed.
—EXODUS 23:12

Most of us don't understand the importance of work. We prefer rest and relaxation to a good day's work. The release of our potential requires that we acknowledge and move beyond the fallacies that characterize our view of work.

SIX DAYS YOU SHALL LABOR...

We are a rest-oriented society. We believe that holidays, vacation and weekends are better than work days. This adoration of time free from work reflects our assumption that rest is to be preferred over work. This is a false assumption. Rest is not better than work.

When God created the world, He worked six days and rested one (see Genesis 2:2). He also instructed us to work six days and rest one (see Exodus 23:12). The result of our desire to work one day and rest six is evident in the boredom and unhappiness that plague our world.

Work always produces more personal growth and satisfaction than rest does. It stirs up your creative abilities and draws from the hidden store of your potential. If you are unfulfilled, you are probably resting too much. You're getting bored because you aren't working. You can't run from work and expect to be happy. Work is the energy that keeps you alive. It's the stuff that gives life meaning. Having six weeks of vacation is not the supreme measure of success or the ultimate prescription for happiness.

RETIREMENT ISN'T PART OF GOD'S PLAN

Sow your seed in the morning, and at evening let not your hands be idle, for you do not know which will succeed, whether this or that, or whether both will do equally well.
—ECCLESIASTES 11:6

A fallacy that affects our view of work is the assumption that retirement is the goal of work. You were not designed to retire. You came out of God, and God hasn't retired. He's been working ever since He spoke the invisible into the visible. Therefore, retirement is not part of His plan for your life. Because God created man by giving him an immortal spirit with eternal potential, God planned enough work to keep you busy forever. Oh, you may retire from a specific organization or job, but you can never retire from life and work. *The minute you quit working, you begin to die, because work is a necessary part of life.*

Have you ever met a retired person who was uncomfortable, bitter, rowdy, and senile? He became that way because He retired from work. The lack of work made him crazy because it took away his means of finding fulfillment.

Just like a car runs on gasoline, you run on work. God created you to feel healthy and happy when you are expending energy to reveal all that He put in you. He designed you to find satisfaction in looking at the fruit of your labor. That's why *inactivity often brings depression and discouragement.* God didn't intend for you to sit around and loaf.

God rested when He became tired. He didn't retire. So He says to you, "I'm still working. Why aren't you? There are still things in you that I need." May God deliver you from the spirit of retirement, because retirement is ungodly, unscriptural, and unbiblical. Retirement is foreign to God's plan for human beings.

Another fallacy that adversely affects your understanding of work is the belief that you can get something for nothing. Nowhere is this fallacy more evident than in our fascination with lotteries. Advertisements for magazine sweepstakes fill our mailboxes. Daily numbers are announced every evening on TV and radio newscasts. Mail-order houses promise great wealth if you buy their products. Get-rich-quick schemes, casinos, and TV game shows captivate millions and feed them this attitude. The messages of our world encourage our desire to get something for nothing. Sadly, we are taken in by their hype. Until we let go of our hideous attempts to receive benefits without effort, we will forfeit the blessings of work, because work is God's pathway to a satisfying, meaningful existence.

You Cannot Fulfill Your Purpose Without Work

...his work will be shown for what it is, because the Day will bring it to light. It will be revealed with fire, and the fire will test the quality of each man's work. If what he has built survives, he will receive his reward.
—1 Corinthians 3:13-14

You cannot fulfill your purpose without work. Trying to get money by winning the lottery bypasses personal fulfillment. Neither can you achieve God's intent for your life by reaping the benefits of someone else's efforts. Those who win the lottery often testify that they are more unhappy after they receive all that money than before. Why? Because they lose their reason for getting up in the morning.

Without purpose, life becomes meaningless. Life on "easy street" is not really easy because satisfaction requires effort. In fact, winning a million dollars could very well kill you if you stopped working. Oh, your body might live for a while, but your potential—the real you—would die from lack of use. The joy of life would be gone.

God gives you work to meet your need for personal fulfillment. When you try to get something for nothing you miss the opportunity to find gratification, because effort is the key to satisfaction. Life bears this out in many ways. *Benefits without work short-circuit fulfillment* because you usually have more appreciation for something you worked hard to get. You remember all you went through to obtain it, and from your remembering flows the impetus to treasure and care for the products of your labor. Handouts meet your desire for material possessions, but they deny you the pride of gaining through effort. This is the weakness of a welfare system that robs the individual of the personal responsibility, gratification and pride that comes from self-development and self-deployment.

Work and Responsibility

Blessed are all who fear the Lord, who walk in his ways. You will eat the fruit of your labor; blessings and prosperity will be yours.
—Psalm 128:1-2

The love of work is the secret to a productive life. *Without work, you will lose direction and gradually succumb to atrophy.* Your very survival will be threatened as the various facets of your life fall apart from a lack of purpose. So crucial is your need to work that the absence of work is often the issue that underlies problems in interpersonal relationships.

If, for example, a man marries without thinking beyond the pleasures of marriage to the responsibilities of a family, he begins to resent those things that naturally go with marriage and the establishment of a home—things like rent, utility bills, car payments, and grocery bills; things like the expenses and obligations that go with children. And, in time, the reasonable responsibilities of a home and a family begin to look unreasonable, and the duties of husband and father become burdens. That's when the problems start, because the man begins to look for a way out of his seemingly intolerable situation. In essence, he begins to call responsibility pressure.

Work is God's way to draw out your potential. Through work He opens the door into your inner storehouse and teaches you how to use your talents and abilities to meet the many responsibilities of life. Work and the ability to handle responsibility go hand in hand because work requires you to take on new challenges, dares you to risk failure to show your capacity for success, and prompts you to take the steps to make your dream a reality.

God wants you to fulfill all that He created you to do and be. That's why He is constantly giving you tasks that reveal more and more of the wealth that lies hidden within you. Little by little, He's chipping away at your storehouse of riches, trying to release all that He put in you. But you must cooperate with His efforts. You must refuse to allow the rest/retirement/I-can-get-something-for-nothing mentality to rob you of your need to work. When you accept your responsibility to work and allow God to change your perceptions of work, you will see a difference in your life because God set work as a priority for personal gratification. Work is the *master key* to releasing your potential.

POTENTIAL IS NEVER REALIZED WITHOUT WORK

For we are God's fellow workers; you are God's field, God's building.
—1 CORINTHIANS 3:9

Have you ever noticed who God uses? God uses busy people. Truly God loves busy people because their busyness shows that they are willing to work. Jesus' preference for busy people is evident in His choice of four fishermen who were preparing their nets, to be His first followers.

The priority Jesus put on work is also evident later in His ministry as He went through the towns and villages of Galilee and Judea, teaching in the synagogues and healing the sick. He saw there many people who were so helpless and harassed that He likened them to sheep without a shepherd. With compassion, He instructed His disciples to pray for workers to meet their needs:

> *Then* [Jesus] *said to His disciples, "The harvest is plentiful but the workers* [laborers] *are few. Ask the Lord of the harvest, therefore, to send workers* [laborers] *into His harvest field"* (Matthew 9:37-38).

Jesus needed *workers.* He needed people who would give their best to bring others into the Kingdom of God. He told His disciples to pray that God would send somebody to work.

Don't Be a Reluctant Worker

One who is slack in his work is brother to one who destroys.
—Proverbs 18:9

When Jesus was on earth, He needed *workers*. He needed people who would give their best to bring others into the Kingdom of God. He told His disciples to pray that God would send somebody to work.

God hasn't changed. Work is still a priority for Him. Nor have the needs of our world changed. Helpless, harassed people still need what God stored in us for them.

But we don't appreciate God's ways. We want results without the process. We seek promotion without responsibility. We desire pay without work. You will not participate in the creative power of the One who says, "I've given you the ability to produce. Now work to see what you can do," until you cease to be a reluctant worker. You must stop refusing to work, unless someone is standing over you, giving you the work, and making sure that you do it. When God commanded Adam to work in the garden, there was no supervisor, manager, or time clock to motivate Adam or to force him to work.

God expects us to understand our natural need to work. The Church, and the world at large, must recover God's principle of work because there can be no greatness without work. We must accept the truth that we need to work because God worked and He created us to work.

GOD WORKED

So on the seventh day He rested from all His work. And God blessed the seventh day and made it holy, because on it He rested from all the work of creating that He had done.
—GENESIS 2:2-3

God set the priority of work when He called the invisible world into view. Before there was anything, there was God. Everything we now see existed first in God, but it was invisible. If God had done nothing to get started, the world we know would not exist. The universe would have stayed inside Him. But God chose to deliver His babies by *working*. He took His potential and, through effort, changed it from potential to experience.

God's efforts in making the world are noteworthy. He determined the number of stars and called them by name (see Psalm 147:4). He covered the sky with clouds, supplied the earth with rain, and made grass to grow on the hills (see Psalm 147:8). He formed the mountains by His power (see Psalm 65:6) and set the foundations of the earth (see Psalm 104:5). The moon marks the seasons by His decree and the sun sets at the appointed time (see Psalm 104:19). So vast and marvelous are God's works in creation that He pronounced them good when He stopped and looked at what He had made. He savored the joy of seeing the wondrous beauty He had brought forth.

> *God saw all that He had made, and it was very good.... Thus the heavens and the earth were completed in all their vast array. By the seventh day God had finished the work He had been doing* (Genesis 1:31-2:2).

God's Effort in Creation

God saw all that He had made, and it was very good. ...Thus the heavens and the earth were completed in all their vast array. By the seventh day God had finished the work He had been doing.
—Genesis 1:31-2:2

God's efforts in making the world are noteworthy. He determined the number of stars and called them by name (see Psalm 147:4). He covered the sky with clouds, supplied the earth with rain, and made grass to grow on the hills (see Psalm 147:8). He formed the mountains by His power see (see Psalm 65:6) and set the foundations of the earth (see Psalm 104:5). The moon marks the seasons by His decree and the sun sets at the appointed time (see Psalm 104:19). So vast and marvelous are God's works in creation that He pronounced them good when He stopped and looked at what He had made. He savored the joy of seeing the wondrous beauty He had brought forth.

God didn't create the world by dreaming, wishing, or imagining. He created it by working. Indeed, God worked so hard that He had to rest.

> *So on the seventh day He rested from all His work. And God blessed the seventh day and made it holy, because on it He rested from all the work of creating that He had done* (Genesis 2:2-3).

Rest is needed after a long, laborious experience, not a tiny task that requires little effort. God's effort in creation was so extensive that He rested.

Too often we think that coming back to God means we don't have to work anymore. How wrong we are! God loves to work. He delights in pulling new things from His Omnipotent Self. He also requires you to work.

GOD CREATED YOU TO WORK

...nor did we eat anyone's food without paying for it. On the contrary, we worked night and day, laboring and toiling so that we would not be a burden to any of you.
—2 THESSALONIANS 3:8

When God created Adam, He gave him dominion. Adam had dominion over:

- Fish (water)
- Birds (air)
- Living creatures (land)

This dominion meant that Adam had to work. Work was an essential part of Adam's life.

The same is true for you. God created you to work. He didn't create you to rest or retire or go on vacation. He didn't create you to punch a time card or to stand under the eagle eye of a boss or supervisor. He gave you birth to experience fulfillment by completing tasks through effort.

Work is a gift from God. Every assignment God has ever given required work. Noah worked to build the ark (see Genesis 6). Joseph worked to provide for the Egyptians during a seven-year famine (see Genesis 41:41ff). Solomon worked to build the Temple (see 2 Chronicles 2-4). As each accomplished what God asked of him, he fulfilled God's purpose for his life. His willingness to do the work God gave him blessed himself and others. Through work these people and many others have met the various responsibilities of their lives.

YOU NEED TO WORK

All hard work brings a profit....
PROVERBS 14:23

Work is honorable. God designed you to meet the needs of your life through work. When you refuse to work, you deny yourself the opportunity to fulfill your purpose, because God created you to act like He acts, and God worked. The release of your potential demands that you admit that you need work.

WORK PROFITS THE WORKER

The plans of the diligent lead to profit (Proverbs 21:5) by providing for physical needs.

> *Make it your ambition to lead a quiet life, to mind your own business and to work with your hands...so that your daily life may win the respect of outsiders and so that you will not be dependent on anybody* (1 Thessalonians 4:11-12).

Work profits the worker by allowing him to meet his financial responsibilities. The apostle Paul provided for his own needs by making tents (see 1 Thessalonians 2:6-9). He did not rely on the provisions of others, but whenever possible, worked for his living.

The same is required of you. Don't become a burden on others. Work to provide for yourself and your family. Settle down and get a job. Put your roots down and do not allow yourself to be easily deterred from your responsibilities. God gave you work to earn the bread you eat.

WORK PROFITS THE WORKER

Do your best to present yourself to God as one approved, a worker who does not need to be ashamed and who correctly handles the Word of truth.
—2 TIMOTHY 2:15

Work profits the worker.

...BY REVEALING POTENTIAL

God also ordained that work would show you your potential. Although all work brings profit, the reward is not always a financial one. You may feel like you are working hard but you're not getting paid what you are worth. Keep working so you can reap the profits of your work. God does not lie. Even if no one ever pays you, your work profits you because you discover what you can do. It is better to deserve an honor and not receive it than to receive an honor and not deserve it.

...BY UNVEILING THE BLESSINGS OF WORK.

Work is much more important than honor because it brings the learning that releases your talents, abilities, and capabilities. It is also more valuable than a paycheck. When you stop working for money, you'll discover the blessing of work.

The laborer's appetite works for him; his hunger drives him on (Proverbs 16:26).

...BY GIVING THE OPPORTUNITY TO REJOICE IN ACHIEVEMENT

A commitment to work will also permit you to develop a perspective that rejoices in achievement more than pay. Then you can find happiness in your work even when the pay is less than what you expect or deserve. Administrators give those who are busy more to do because they know the busy people are willing to work. *If you want to be promoted, get busy. Become productive.* When you work, work because you want to know what you can do, not because you are trying to get paid. You may not be noticed immediately, but your promotion will come. Excellent work always profits the worker.

...BY BUILDING SELF-ESTEEM.

Finally, work profits you by enhancing your self-esteem. If you feel worthless, find some work. Get busy. When you have something to do, your ability to feel good about yourself can change overnight. As you take the opportunity to focus on the results of your labor instead of the losses in your life that tempt you to feel unloveable and incapable, your estimation of yourself will grow. Work keeps you healthy, physically and emotionally.

SO WHO'S STEALING?

...I have never seen the righteous forsaken or their children begging bread. They are always generous and lend freely; their children will be blessed.
—PSALM 37:25-26

If I were to ask you to describe a thief, you would probably talk about someone who entered your home and took your possessions. This is certainly a legitimate definition, but the thief doesn't always have to sneak in and out to take what isn't his.

Many of us go to work and steal from our bosses. We come to work late, take extra long lunch hours, and go home early. Or we take home the pencils, paper, pens, and paper clips that belong to the company, we make private copies on the boss's copy machine, and we conduct personal business on company time. These actions are no better than those of a thief who enters your home and takes your possessions because both result in the loss of goods that someone else worked to provide.

In an even broader sense, a thief is anyone who relies on the productiveness of another to provide for his needs because he is too lazy to meet them himself. If you are able to work and you're not working, you are stealing from those who are working. You're requiring them to provide what you could get for yourself if you would work. If you are eating but not working, or you are living in a house but not working, you are a thief. *Taking the benefits of work without participating in the effort is theft.*

THE PENALTIES OF LAZINESS—PART 1

Even when we were with you, we gave you this rule:
"If a man will not work, he shall not eat."
—2 THESSALONIANS 3:10

Sitting around is no more acceptable to God than taking what does not belong to you. You rob yourself and others when you are lazy. Like any theft, laziness carries many penalties. The first of these is *hunger*:

> *The sluggard craves and gets nothing, but the desires of the diligent are fully satisfied* (Proverbs 13:4).
>
> *Laziness brings on deep sleep, and the shiftless man goes hungry* (Proverbs 19:15).

A second penalty of laziness is *isolation* and *shame*:

> *In the name of the Lord Jesus Christ, we command you, brothers, to keep away from every brother who is idle. ...Do not associate with him, in order that he may feel ashamed* (2 Thessalonians 3:6,14).
>
> *A poor man is shunned by all his relatives—how much more do his friends avoid him!* (Proverbs 19:7).

A third penalty of laziness is *others' reluctance to take you seriously*, because lazy people always have an excuse why they aren't working.

> *The sluggard says, "There is a lion outside!" or, "I will be murdered in the streets!"* (Proverbs 22:13).

THE PENALTIES OF LAZINESS—PART 2

Do you see a man skilled in his work? He will serve before kings; he will not serve before obscure men.
—PROVERBS 22:29

Like any theft, laziness carries many penalties. The first of these is *hunger.* A second penalty of laziness is *isolation* and *shame.* A third penalty of laziness is *others' reluctance to take you seriously*, because lazy people always have an excuse why they aren't working.

A fourth penalty of laziness is *lost opportunities for advancement* because jealousy and over-concern for the progress of others prevents you from doing your work.

> *Be sure you know the condition of your flocks, give careful attention to your herds; for riches do not endure forever and a crown is not secure for all generations* (Proverbs 27:23-24).

A fifth penalty of laziness is *the inability to see your own need to get up and work*:

> *The sluggard is wiser in his own eyes than seven men who answer discreetly* (Proverbs 26:16).

A sixth penalty of laziness is an increasing *loss of ambition*:

> *The sluggard buries his hand in the dish; he is too lazy to bring it back to his mouth* (Proverbs 26:15).

> *Go to the ant, you sluggard; consider its ways and be wise! It has no commander, no overseer or ruler, yet it stores its provisions in summer and gathers it food at harvest* (Proverbs 6:6-8).

A seventh penalty of laziness is the *desire to sleep*:

> *As a door turns on its hinges, so a sluggard turns on his bed* (Proverbs 26:14).

An eighth penalty of laziness is *the inability to take pride in what you have accomplished* because you haven't accomplished anything.

> *The lazy man does not roast his game, but the diligent man prizes his possessions* (Proverbs 12:27).

A ninth penalty of laziness is *slavery*:

> *Diligent hands will rule, but laziness ends in slave labor* (Proverbs 12:24).

An tenth penalty of laziness, and the most severe, is *poverty*. Poverty is the cumulative result of all the other penalties.

> *All hard work brings a profit, but mere talk leads only to poverty* (Proverbs 14:23).

The Most Severe Penalty for Laziness—Poverty

Go to the ant, you sluggard; consider its ways and be wise! It has no commander, no overseer or ruler, yet it stores its provisions in summer and gathers its food at harvest.
—Proverbs 6:6-8

A tenth penalty of laziness, and the most severe, is *poverty*. Poverty is the cumulative result of all the other penalities.

> *All hard work brings a profit, but mere talk leads only to poverty* (Proverbs 14:23).
>
> *How long will you lie there, you sluggard? When will you get up from your sleep? A little sleep, a little slumber, a little folding of the hands to rest—and poverty will come on you like a bandit and scarcity like an armed man* (Proverbs 6:9-11).
>
> *Lazy hands make a man poor...* (Proverbs 10:4).

A sluggard is a lazy bum—my mother used to call them "grassy bellies." When I was young I didn't understand what my mom meant. But one day when I was sitting in the library at the university I realized that Mom called sluggards grassy bellies because they lay on their bellies long enough for grass to grow on them. The Greek word for *poor*, as used by Jesus, is *poucos*, which means "nonproductivity." That's what poverty is. To be poor doesn't mean you don't *have* anything. It means you aren't *doing* anything.

Poverty is cured by hard work. If you don't work you will end up begging. Or you'll become a slave to your boss because you refuse to work for your own satisfaction in completing the job and wait for him to force you to work.

Look at the birds. God provides food for them, but they have to go and look for it. They have to dig and pull it out of the ground. So it is with you. God has given you many talents and ambitions to bring satisfaction and fulfillment into your life. But you have to go and look for that fulfillment. You can't sit back and wait for it to come to you, because it will never come. Work is God's path to an abundant, fulfilling life that reveals the wealth of your potential. *God established your need to work when He worked out His potential in creation and demanded the same of Adam.*

GOD'S DEFINITION OF WORK

Why spend money on what is not bread, and your labor on what does not satisfy? Listen, listen to me, and eat what is good, and your soul will delight in the richest of fare.
—ISAIAH 55:2

Our definition of work and God's are very different. Work is not the same as a job. Work releases potential; a job provides a paycheck. While you may work at your job, work does not always result in a financial reward. Work arises out of a desire to contribute to the world's wealth and well-being by giving of yourself. It moves beyond effort under the force of another and avoids the "I'm not going to work because you can't make me work" mentality.

Frequently we make work overly sophisticated. We need to get labor back into work. We need to *labor* in the office, not just go to the office. God didn't say, "Six days you shall go to your job," but "six days you shall work." Until we change our attitude toward work we will not obey this commandment.

Labor isn't so much *doing things* as *delivering hidden stuff.* It's delivering the babies you will die with if you don't work them into sight. It doesn't matter what kind of job you have, whether you are an executive, a salesman, a factory worker, or a housewife. Work as though your life depended on it, because it does.

Jesus commanded us to pray for *laborers.* This term is also used to describe the process of a woman in childbearing. The process of delivering the pride and joy of a new baby—the hidden potential—involves conception, time, development, adjustments, labor, pain, and cooperation. All are necessary for the manifestation of a child. This process is the same for all humanity. Labor delivers!

Work is God's way of revealing your talents, abilities, and capabilities. It helps you to discover the satisfaction of accomplishment and the results of perseverance. Without work you'll never see the results of your potential. Without effort you'll never feel the satisfaction of accomplishment.

Work Is Bringing Something to Pass

And we pray this in order that you may live a life worthy of the Lord and may please Him in every way: bearing fruit in every good work, growing in the knowledge of God.
—Colossians 1:10

A fantasy is a dream without labor. It is also a vision without a mission. When God gives the potential for something, He also demands that it be worked out. The story of Abraham is a good example of this principle.

One day when God and Abraham were on top of a mountain, God told Abraham that He would give him everything as far as he could see to the north, south, east, and west. Then God told him to *walk* the length and breadth of the land to *receive* what he had been promised (Genesis 13:14-17). Along with the promise came the command to work. Before Abraham could take possession of his inheritance, he had to fight those who lived in the land. The promise would not be possession without effort.

The same is true for you. Every time God gives you a promise, He also gives you the command to work to receive what He has promised. God doesn't just deliver like Santa Claus. You have to fight to get what is yours. The potential to possess what God has given is within you, but you will not obtain the promise until you put forth the effort to claim it.

So if you need money to pay your bills, don't wait for someone to drop the dollars into your hand. Get up and take the job God sends.

Every job, no matter how much you dislike it, is working for you. If you can educate yourself to work no matter what the conditions are, you will learn discipline, because the work is more important than the conditions. Work is also more important than the job. If a child always gets what he wants, he learns to expect his wants to be met without any effort on his part. Our world is full of adults who act like spoiled children. They never learned the value of work.

We do well when we learn the lesson early in life that God requires us to work for what we want. One of the greatest things parents can do for their children is to demand that they learn the responsibility of work at an early age. If your child has to work for his spending money, he will soon learn that he can't get something for nothing. *Work brings potential to pass.* Without work, all you have is potential.

How to Work Out Your Potential

The plans of the diligent lead to profit as
surely as haste leads to poverty.
—Proverbs 21:5

Are you hungry to accomplish something? Are you so committed to a vision that you will do anything to see that vision come to life? Then make plans and follow them.

There's a difference between plans and haste. Haste is trying to get something for nothing. Haste leads to poverty. But the hard worker make plans and expends the effort to see those plans pay off.

Do you want to be a lawyer, a doctor, a teacher, a carpenter, a policeman, a minister, a secretary, an accountant, or a politician? Put some work behind that dream. Burn the midnight oil and study. Make the acquaintance of a person who is working in your chosen field and work with him to learn the trade, business, or profession. The completion of your plans is related to your willingness to work, as is your prosperity. Likewise, *the release of your potential is dependent upon your expenditure of the necessary effort to change your thoughts into visible realities. Work of your own initiative. Don't wait for life to force you to work.*

Work is the key to your personal progress, productivity, and fulfillment. Without work you can accomplish nothing. God assigns you work so you can release your possibilities and abilities by putting forth the effort to accomplish each task. The responsibilities

God gives you are presented to provoke your potential and to challenge you to try new things. Until you stop being a reluctant worker, you will miss the vitality and meaning that God intended work to bring to your life.

Accept today God's gracious gift of work. Refuse to allow a pessimistic attitude toward work to rob you of your potential. Then look forward to the joy of accomplishment and the delight of discovering all God put in you for the world. You will truly find that work is a blessing.

THE DEFINITION OF RESPONSIBILITY

The disciples, each according to his ability, decided to provide help for the brothers living in Judea.
—ACTS 11:29

I am convinced that life was designed to create environments that make demands on our potential. Without these demands our potential would lie dormant. This thought is reflected in the saying, "Necessity is the mother of invention." How true! Most of us respond to life creatively and innovatively only when circumstances *demand* that response. The many technological, medical, and social breakthroughs that have been achieved because problems or circumstances demanded a response vividly illustrate this truth. The Book of Genesis also clearly reveals this principle in the account of man's first encounter with creation in the Garden of Eden.

Man, as God first created him, was one hundred percent unreleased potential. He was an adult with full capabilities, talents, and gifts. His physical, mental, intellectual, emotional, and spiritual powers were fully developed. But man's powers and abilities were totally unused, untapped, unmanifested, unchallenged, and unemployed. The Creator's plan for releasing this hidden ability is recorded in Genesis 2:15,19-20.

God's first action after creating this totally new man—a man with muscles that had never been exercised, a brain that had never been stimulated, emotions that had never been aroused, an imagination that had never been ignited, and creativity that had never been explored—was to give him assignments that placed demands on his hidden abilities. By giving Adam's ability responsibility, God placed demands on Adam's potential. In a similar manner, your potential is released when demands to fulfill an assignment in God's greater purpose for your life are placed on you. This is why *work* is called *employment*—it employs your abilities for the purpose of manifesting your potential.

DYING EMPTY

*For I testify that they gave as much as they were able,
and even beyond their ability. Entirely on their own....*
—2 CORINTHIANS 8:3

God's command to *work* required Adam to use his physical potential. Likewise, God's commands to *cultivate the garden* and to *name the animals* activated his intellectual, mental, and creative potential. The demands God makes on you accomplish the same thing in your life. The release of your potential demands that you accept the responsibility to work, because the greatest need of ability is responsibility. You will never know the extent of your potential until you give it something to do. The greatest tragedy in your life will not be your death, but what dies with you at death. What a shame to waste what God gave you to use.

Have you ever noticed the deep peace and contentment that come over you when you fulfill a responsibility? Nothing is more rewarding and personally satisfying than the successful completion of an assigned task. The joy and elation that fill you at such times are the fruit of achievement. The experience of fulfillment is directly related to this principle of *finishing*.

An old Chinese proverb says: "The end of a thing is greater than its beginning." In other words, finishing is more important than starting. The beginning of a task may bring a degree of anxiety and apprehension, but the completing of a task usually yields a sense of relief, joy, and fulfillment.

History is filled with great starters who died unfinished. In fact, the majority of the five billion human beings who inhabit the earth will die unfinished. What a tragedy! What counts is not how much a person starts, but how much he or she finishes. The race is not to the swift, but to him that endures to the end.

THE PURPOSE OF YOUR POTENTIAL

OUR MAIN GOAL

Who endowed the heart with wisdom or
gave understanding to the mind?
—JOB 38:36

The potential of everything is related to its purpose for being. Before we can understand the potential of a thing or person, we first must know the conditions under which it was meant to exist. Thus the most important thing for you and me, as human beings, is to try and find out for the rest of our lives what is the purpose for everything in life. That is our main goal. Unless we ask ourselves, "What is the purpose for everything in life?" we will die without having experienced the potential of everything. We will miss the wisdom of God in creation.

The apostle Paul, in the first chapter of First Corinthians, describes the wisdom of the world and the wisdom of God.

> *Where is the wise man? Where is the scholar? Where is the philosopher of this age? has not God made foolish the wisdom of the world? For since in the wisdom of God the world through its wisdom did not know Him, God was pleased through the foolishness of what was preached to save those who believe. Jews demand miraculous signs and Greeks look for wisdom, but we preach Christ crucified: a stumbling block to Jews and foolishness to Gentiles* (1 Corinthians 1:20-23).

When somebody tells you they are wise, don't get carried away. Although they may have wisdom, it might not be the right kind of wisdom.

Born to Expose His Nature

...the people I formed for myself that they may proclaim my praise.
—Isaiah 43:21

Not only did God carefully plan for the details of your life, He also determined how your life would fit into His total plan for man. Part of the answer to the why of our birth is revealed in God's desire that we should show forth His glory. The glory of God is the excess of His nature. It's all the potential of our omnipotent God that has not yet been revealed. He's full of so much more than we can think or imagine and He's waiting to use us to realize that potential.

> *Now to Him who is able to do immeasurably more than all we ask or imagine, according to His power that is at work within us, to Him be glory in the church and in Christ Jesus throughout all generations, for ever and ever! Amen* (Ephesians 3:20-21).

Throughout the Bible, God tells us to make His name great in the earth. Praise and thanks are due God's name, which is great and awesome (see Psalm 44:8; 99:3). His name is to be proclaimed among the nations (see Malachi 1:11) as well as in Israel (see Psalm 76:1). His name is holy (see Luke 1:49; Psalm 99:3) and mighty in power (see Jeremiah 10:6). Everything is done for "His name's sake." To understand this concept, we must also understand that the Hebrew concept of "name" literally is synonymous with the object. In other words, the name of the thing is the thing. Therefore, the name of God is Himself, and He is His name. To glorify His name, then, means exposing His nature.

God created *you* to bring glory to His name. His predestined plan for *your* life was designed to bring Him glory. He knows there is more to you than we can see because He placed part of Himself in you. His plan for your life is part of His creative work—through you God wants to continue the birth of His potential. Because you share God's omnipotent nature, Jesus said you can do even greater things than He did, if you only believe (see Mark 11:23).

SPIRITS CANNOT DIE

After that, we who are still alive and are left will be caught up together with them in the clouds to meet the Lord in the air. And so we will be with the Lord forever.
—1 THESSALONIANS 4:17

One day as I was talking with the Holy Spirit, He said to me, "Myles, what are you?"

I said, "Spirit."

He said, "Yea! You got that down! Do you know that spirits cannot die?"

I said, "This is true."

Then He said, "Why do humans think in terms of time only? I came back to earth to introduce humans to eternity."

I said, "Whoa!"

Then the Holy Spirit showed me how God had designed us to live forever. He said, "If you have to live forever, which you will, what are you going to do? God intended you to live forever because spirits never die. And you have to live forever being fulfilled. God never makes anything without a purpose. So you are designed to live forever and you've got to be fulfilling your purpose in life. God had to make sure He stored enough in you to last forever so you will never get bored."

That blew my mind. We are going to live forever.

Sometimes we sing: "When I get to Heaven I'm going to praise the Lord for a thousand years."

"What are you going to do after that?"

"Well, then I'll walk around the streets of gold for another thousand years."

"What are you going to do after that?" You have eternity to live. After a million years of worshiping and bowing and keeping company with the angels, what are you going to do? Your mind is so small. You think, "Wow. Look what I have accomplished."

God says, "Gosh, your life is a spot in eternity—just a drop in eternity. You will not begin really living until you leave time and enter eternity."

God has packed so much into you that the book He wrote on you is only the book for time. Your potential from birth to death is contained in that book—a book so full of expectations that David says it is "vast."

CREATED FOR ETERNAL LIFE

Lord, you have been our dwelling place
throughout all generations.
—PSALM 90:1

God is called a creator because He always has something to do. God is always busy doing something. When God took us out of Himself, He gave us part of His Spirit. God is Spirit and spirits are eternal. They cannot die. Therefore, what is spirit and comes out of God is also eternal. When God created human beings, He said, "This one will keep Us excited forever. Let's make and create a being in Our own image. Let's make one who will not fade away." Mountains will fade away and rivers will run dry. Streams will evaporate and the oceans will go away. But when God came up with man, He created something that would last forever. He took man out of Himself. God made you spirit and put so much stuff in you that it will take an eternal life to live it all. *Your true potential requires eternal life to be realized and maximized.*

There is no retirement in the Bible. Why? Because God knows you have eternity to go just like He does. God wants you to assist Him in creating and developing and dominating and ruling forever and ever and ever. That's a long time. The wealth of your potential is so rich it requires an eternal life to bring it out.

We are not going to be in Heaven for a million years bowing down around a throne. God doesn't have an ego problem. He doesn't need us to tell Him how nice He is. In fact, He was nice without us. We make Him look pretty bad. We've really messed up God. We came out of God. We are the only ones made in His image, and look what we did. God was better off without us. He doesn't need our praises to make Him feel high.

God has placed enough potential in you to last forever. Try to do as much now as you can. Pack as much as you can into the 70 to 100 years you have here. Go for it. Go for a hunk of gold. Go for the mountain that has the gold in it. Go for the whole thing. Because if you can think it, you can do it. God is the limit of your ability. He won't allow you to think it if you can't do it.

GOD'S PURPOSE FOR MAN: ACTING LIKE GOD

Through these He has given us His very great and precious promises, so that through them you may participate in the divine nature and escape the corruption in the world caused by evil desires.
—2 PETER 1:4

The Bible clearly defines God's reasons for creating human beings:

- To express God's image.
- To enjoy fellowship with God.
- To dominate the earth.
- To bear fruit.
- To reproduce ourselves.

Expressing God's image has to do with the way you act, not the way you look. He wants you to mirror His character. He fashioned you so that His nature could be revealed through your uniqueness.

The essence of God's nature is succinctly defined in the "love" chapter we looked at earlier. He is the wonderful things this chapter describes.

> [God] *is patient,* [God] *is kind. [He] does not envy,* [He] *does not boast,* [He] *is not proud. [God] is not rude,* [He] *is not self-seeking,* [He] *is not easily angered,* [He] *keeps no*

> *record of wrongs. God does not delight in evil but rejoices with the truth.* [God] *always protects, always trusts, always hopes, always perseveres.* [God] *never fails* (1 Corinthians 13:4-8).

This is how you were created to live. God made you to act like He does. Having God's nature is the difference between *looking* lovely and *being* lovely. One refers to your outward appearance, the other to your nature. You may look good, but be mean. You may dress nicely, but speak unkindly. You may look religious, but act like the devil. God wants you to express His nature. That's one reason He created you.

GOD'S PURPOSE FOR MAN: DOMINATING THE EARTH

You have made him to have dominion over the works of Your hands; You have put all things under his feet.
—PSALM 8:6 NKJV

We are continuing to study God's reasons for creating human beings:

- To express God's image.
- To enjoy fellowship with God.
- To dominate the earth.
- To bear fruit.
- To reproduce ourselves.

The Genesis description of man's creation includes God's intent that man should have dominion over the earth:

> *Then God said, "Let Us make man in Our image, in Our likeness, and let them rule over the fish of the sea and the birds of the air, over the livestock, over all the earth, and over all the creatures that move along the ground"* (Genesis 1:26).

God created us to dominate the entire earth. But when we lost touch with our Source, we became confused and allowed the earth to dominate us. Every problem that we are experiencing is the result of our not fulfilling our purpose to dominate the earth.

We've allowed ourselves to be so dominated by leaves and fruit that they tell us what to do. "It's time for a smoke now. You can't do without me."

But more serious than the domination itself is the deception that goes along with the domination. We are tremendous self-deceivers. Social drinkers say, "I can hold my liquor. I'm not under any pressure to have another drink." But the truth is that every alcoholic started as a social drinker.

When we become dominated by the things we were supposed to dominate, all the earth goes off course. Our world is filled with the violence that revolves around the printed paper that comes from trees. *Money* controls our lives. We kill, rob, steal, cuss, and do many other despicable things to get our hands on that sliver of wood.

Even as the domination of people by things destroys our world, so too the domination of people by people creates pain and violence. Husbands abuse their wives. Women abuse their children. Races discriminate against other races. These problems and many more arise from our failure to understand that God gave us dominion over the earth, not over other people.

GOD'S PURPOSE FOR MAN: BEARING FRUIT

This is to My Father's glory, that you bear much fruit, showing yourselves to be My disciples. ...You did not choose Me, but I chose you and appointed you to go and bear fruit—fruit that will last....
—JOHN 15:8,16

Review God's reasons for creating human beings:

- To express God's image.
- To enjoy fellowship with God.
- To dominate the earth.
- To bear fruit.
- To reproduce ourselves.

If you have an apple tree in your backyard that never produces any apples, you're going to get tired of that tree taking up space without bearing any fruit and you'll cut it down. The same is true of God's relationships with people. No tree should ever be without fruit, because God created every tree with its seed inside it. God has a way of moving unproductive people to the side and raising up productive people. *A productive person is simply somebody who will respond to the demand.*

Jesus teaches us in the Gospel of John that God created us to bear fruit (see above).

Your fruitfulness is related to the food you are eating. If your spiritual source is not of top quality, your productivity will show it. No matter where you go or what you do, apart from God you will be an ornamental plant without fruit. You are what you eat.

God wants you to reveal all the potential He buried inside you. He offers you tremendous opportunities to share in His work on this earth. Your ability to fulfill God's demand is connected to your relationship with Him because the fruitfulness He desires is the manifestation of His Spirit in your life:

> *But the fruit of the Spirit is love, joy, peace, patience, kindness, goodness, faithfulness, gentleness and self-control. Against such things there is no law. Those who belong to Christ Jesus have crucified the sinful nature with its passions and desires. Since we live by the Spirit, let us keep in step with the Spirit* (Galatians 5:22-25).

God created you to bear abundant, life-giving fruit. That's part of your purpose. The presence of the Holy Spirit in your life is the key to fulfilling that purpose.

GOD'S PURPOSE FOR MAN: REPRODUCING OURSELVES

Anyone who believes in the Son of God has this testimony in his heart. Anyone who does not believe God has made him out to be a liar, because he has not believed the testimony God has given about His Son.
—1 JOHN 5:10

We continue to study God's reasons for creating human beings:

- To express God's image.
- To enjoy fellowship with God.
- To dominate the earth.
- To bear fruit.
- To reproduce ourselves.

God created you to multiply and replenish the earth (see Genesis 1:28). This ability to have children is sometimes seen as a curse rather than a blessing. Sin is at the root of these feelings.

When God gave Adam and Eve the command to fill the earth, pain was not associated with childbearing. It was not until after sin entered the world that God told the woman:

> *...I will greatly increase your pains in childbearing; with pain you will give birth to children. Your desire will be for your husband, and he will rule over you* (Genesis 3:16).

But more important that your ability to physically reproduce is your power to instill in others your values and attitudes. Your life influences your children, your spouse, your friends, your boss, your coworkers, and so on, for good or evil. They watch your actions and hear your words. The effect of your presence in their lives can be either encouraging or discouraging, upbuilding or degrading, positive or negative.

What (or Who) Is Controlling You?

...who, by the power that enables Him to bring everything under His control, will transform our lowly bodies so that they will be like His glorious body.
—Philippians 3:21

The release of your potential is directly related to your willingness to know, understand, and submit to God's purposes for your life. The wisdom and power to accomplish this task is available to all who have the gift of God's indwelling Spirit. For He is the channel through which you can freely communicate with God until your heart and vision become one with His.

The corollary is also true. Life apart from God subjects you to control by other things, people, and spirits and conceals the purpose for which you were born. Under those circumstances, you and your potential will be abused. Indeed, much that you have to offer will die with you.

Take time now to examine your life. Who or what is controlling you? Are you releasing your potential by discovering God's purpose for your life?

You have the ability to fulfill that purpose because God built it into you. Determine now to find God's intent for your life.

THE PRINCIPLE OF FINISHING

For I am already being poured out like a drink offering, and the time has come for my departure. I have fought a good fight, I have finished my race, I have kept the faith.
—2 TIMOTHY 4:6-7

Jesus finished His task on earth. The words He spoke on the Cross clearly indicate that He fulfilled an assignment, completed a task and satisfied a requirement. They resonate with a deep sense of peace. In fact, they confirm that He was not killed but simply died.

> *When He had received the drink, Jesus said, "It is finished." With that, He bowed His head and gave up His spirit* (John 19:30).

Because He had released and maximized His potential to successfully fulfill the purpose for which God had sent Him into the world, Jesus saw death not as something to be feared, but as the natural next step. In other words, Jesus went to the grave empty.

This principle of *finishing* is also expressed very clearly by the apostle Paul in his second letter to Timothy (see above).

Paul faced death with complete confidence and peace because he knew that he had fulfilled God's purpose for his life. When he spoke of being "poured out," which suggests emptying some contents from oneself, he pointed to an accurate and important concept that must be understood by all who would release their potential.

You, like Paul and our Lord Jesus Christ, were born for a purpose. The ability to fulfill that purpose resides deep inside you screaming to be released. Perhaps you yearn to write books, compose songs, scribe poetry, obtain an academic degree, paint on canvas, play music, open a business, serve in a political, civic or spiritual organization, visit other countries, or develop an invention. Think how long you've carried your dream. Recall how many times you have postponed satisfying your desire. Count the many times you began to realize your goal only to quit.

God did not intend that the cemetery would be the resting place of your potential. The grave irresponsibility of taking your precious dreams, visions, ideas, and plans to the grave is not part of His design. You have a responsibility to release your potential. Join Jesus, Paul, and many others who robbed death of the pleasure of aborting their potential. Remember, the wealth of the cemetery is the potential of the unfinished.

DON'T WASTE YOUR POTENTIAL, SHARE IT

DON'T WAIT TO BE CHALLENGED

And God is able to make all grace abound to you, so that in all things at all times, having all that you need, you will abound in every good work.
—2 CORINTHIANS 9:8

God has promised that He can do far more than you can think or imagine. His power is available to you. Is that power working in you? Are you saying to God: "I've got some power, now work it for me. Give me something to do"?

God has given you a skill or ability the world needs. He has been waiting for your birth. Perhaps He planted within you a unique ability to work for life. Imagine a dead baby turning purple in your hand. Others are thinking "undertaker," but you know that God has given you a potential to restore life. You believe God and pray, by the power of His Spirit, "God, this dear baby must live." Even though someone might overhear you, and that makes your prayer all the more difficult, you tap into the potential God planted deep within you and believe for the baby's life.

God has given you a skill or ability the world needs.

Miracles happen when we give our potential responsibility. God designed it that way. Don't allow the things within you to die with you because you did not challenge them. God planted the seed of potential within you. He made you according to the *potential principle*—like the rest of His creation. Don't waste that gift. Give your potential some responsibility.

Receiving and Releasing

Guard the good deposit that was entrusted to you—guard it with the help of the Holy Spirit who lives in us.
—2 Timothy 1:14

Everything in creation was designed to function on the simple principle of receiving and releasing. Life depends on this principle. What if the plants refused to release the oxygen they possess or if we human beings refused to release the carbon dioxide we produce? The result would be chaos and death for the entire planet. Unreleased potential is not only useless, it is dangerous—both for the person or thing who failed to release it and for everything that lives with them. Dormant potential is not healthy, advantageous, safe or effective. You must understand that your valuable deposit of potential was given to enrich the lives of others. When potential is kept, it self-destructs.

The tremendous potential you and I have been given is locked inside us, waiting for demands to be made on it. We have a responsibility to use what God stored in us for the good of the world. We dare not leave this planet with it. Many of us are aware of the ability we have inside, but we have been frustrated by our failure to release that ability. Some of us blame our historical circumstances. Others blame social status. Still others transfer the responsibility for their failure and frustration to their lack of formal education or their less than ideal opportunities.

Over the years, I have come to realize that no excuse *can* be given to justify the destruction of the seed of potential that God placed within you. You *can* become the man or woman you were born to be. You *can* accomplish the vision you saw. You *can* build that business you planned. You *can* develop that school you imagine. *You* are the only one who can stop you. No matter what your environment, you have the ability to change your attitude and your internal environment until they are conducive to the germination of your potential seed. You must not add to the wealth of the graveyard. You owe it to the next generation to live courageously so the treasure of your potential is unleashed. The world needs what God deposited in you for the benefit of your contemporaries and all the generations to follow.

YOU CAN BE FRUITFUL AND MULTIPLY

By their fruit you will recognize them. Do people pick grapes from thornbushes, or figs from thistles?
—MATTHEW 7:16

God's perspective on our potential includes dominating, ruling and subduing the earth. His perspective also sees our potential to multiply. God gave every human being the potential to be fruitful and to reproduce after their kind.

> *God blessed them and said to them, "Be fruitful and increase in number; fill the earth and subdue it. Rule over the fish of the sea and the birds of the air and over every living creature that moves on the ground* (Genesis 1:28).

While it is true that God gave us the ability to have children, the potential God is talking about here is much more than the capacity to have babies. He has given men and women the potential to reproduce what they are. We are producing the next generation.

What kind of children are you producing? God has given you the power to influence them either for good or for evil. Will the next generation be cussing, alcoholic, illiterate people? Or will they be righteous and upright, seeking the Lord and obeying His commandments? You have the capacity to produce children who mirror your life.

Work Blesses Others

Share with God's people who are in need. Practice hospitality.
—Romans 12:13

Work affords the opportunity to help others. Indeed, the Gospel of Matthew records a parable in which our willingness to help meet the needs of others is the basis on which our faithfulness or unfaithfulness to Christ is judged (see Matthew 25:31-46). The apostle Paul notes the benefits of sharing when he commends the Corinthian church for their willingness to help sister churches in need (see 2 Corinthians 8-9). He advises them to give generously, not grudgingly, with the promise that what they give and more will be returned to them:

> *Remember this: Whoever sows sparingly will also reap sparingly, and whoever sows generously will also reap generously. Each man should give what he has decided in his heart to give, not reluctantly or under compulsion, for God loves a cheerful giver. ...Now He who supplies seed to the sower and bread for food will also supply and increase your store of seed and will enlarge the harvest of your righteousness. You will be made rich in every way so that you can be generous on every occasion...* (2 Corinthians 9:6-7,10-11).

POTENTIAL IS NEVER GIVEN FOR ITSELF

Therefore, as we have opportunity, let us do good to all people, especially to those who belong to the family of believers.
—GALATIONS 6:10

When I was in college, I went on a tour of Europe. After several days, I lost interest in all I was seeing because my fiancée, who is now my wife, was not there to share it with me. On that trip I learned the truth of this principle: *Potential is never given for itself. Whatever God gives to you, He gives for others.*

Even as a solitary instrument cannot produce the majestic music of a symphonic orchestra, so human beings cannot glorify their Creator in isolation. I need your potential to maximize mine, and you need my potential to maximize yours. All we have been given is meant to be shared.

After man had finished naming all the animals and no suitable helper for him was found among them, God performed another significant act of creation. Why? "*It is not good for the man to be alone*" (Genesis 2:18).

God did not make woman because man asked for a wife, nor because a helper for man was a good idea. Man *needed* a companion because he could not realize his potential without sharing it with someone. His solitary existence was not good.

To be solitary or alone is not the same as being single. To be alone is to be isolated and cut off from others. Communication is impossible because you have no one like yourself to share with. This is what God says is not good.

To be single is to be unmarried. Marriage is not a requirement or a prerequisite for the fulfillment of your potential. You do not necessarily *need* a husband or a wife. What you do need, however, is someone with whom you can share your potential. This is true because *your personal satisfaction is connected to your fulfilling God's purpose for your life, and your purpose cannot be achieved in isolation.* You need those people who will call forth your potential and into whom you can pour your life. *You may be wired to be single, but you are not designed to live isolated and alone.*

GIVING EXPOSES POTENTIAL

In everything I did, I showed you that by this kind of hard work we must help the weak, remembering the words the Lord Jesus himself said: 'It is more blessed to give than to receive.'"
—ACTS 20:35

Treasures that are hidden and locked up benefit no one. Say, for example, that your grandmother gave you a beautiful necklace that she wore as a bride. If you keep it locked in a safe and never wear it, its beauty is wasted.

Or perhaps you have wedding gifts of beautiful china, sterling silver, and fine crystal that you have never used to serve a meal. You're wasting the potential of those dishes. They cannot do what they are supposed to do sitting on a shelf. People bought them for you to use. *Treasure is useless unless you expose it.* Potential can never be attained if it has no opportunity to give.

This was the power of John F. Kennedy's words, spoken at his inauguration to be the president of the United States: "Ask not what your country can do for you, but what you can do for your country." Kennedy's words prompt us to focus on what we can give instead of what we can get. It is through our giving that we discover what we can do and be.

This was also the wisdom shared by the apostle Paul, "*It is more blessed to give than to receive*" (Acts 20:35). Releasing what you have received benefits you and others. Holding on to a treasure forfeits the blessing inherit in the treasure, and no one profits from it.

Like the seed, *you must release what God has stored in you for the world.* You do this by releasing seeds into the soil of the lives of others.

GOD IS A GIVER

How great is the love the Father has lavished on us, that we should be called children of God! And that is what we are! The reason the world does not know us is that it did not know Him.
—1 JOHN 3:1

God is constantly releasing seeds into the soil of your life. He is a giver and He created you to be like Him. The foundation of God's giving nature is revealed in His purpose for creating men and women.

God made Adam and Eve so He would have someone to love and bless—more children like Christ, His Incarnate Son. Although God possessed all He had created, those things were useless to Him until He created man to release their potential by using His creations and, thereby, showing off His fullness.

In essence, God, who is love, created man to fulfill His potential to love. Love is worthless until it is given away. It must have an object to be fulfilled. Therefore, God needed something on which He could lavish His love, something that could understand and appreciate what He had to give. Of all God's creatures, only men and women share God's Spirit and, thus, can appreciate His love.

You are the object of God's love. Because love can be fulfilled only when the receiver of love is like the giver, He created you like Himself, to be loved by Him and to love as He loves.

BEAT THE ODDS

I have told you these things, so that in Me you may have peace. In this world you will have trouble. But take heart! I have overcome the world.
—JOHN 16:33

Men and women who make changes in history are those who have come against the odds and told the odds it is impossible for the odds to stop them. Don't throw yourself away—don't let anyone else throw you away because you are up against some odds.

The minute we see somebody in a wheelchair something happens to us. We think the person is half a person. We almost treat him as if we apologize for his condition. We look at people who are blind...who have a withered hand...who walk with a limp...who have only one arm as though they are half a person. We limit their potential to the wheelchair or the limp or the missing hand or the short arm. We reduce everybody to their bodies. You are not your body. Some of the greatest minds in the world are in wheelchairs.

I think about President Roosevelt in a wheelchair. Did you ever think an invalid could be the president of one of the greatest nations on earth?

Suppose you end up in a wheelchair next year with all the brains you have right now. Will you quit? Is your dream related to your body? Don't say "no" too fast. Some of you would just quit and get totally depressed and so sad. You'd say, "Oh, life didn't work out for me," and you'd allow all the dreams you have right now to die in the chair. You'd simply quit.

Don't give up because you are physically handicapped. Don't give up if you are facing great odds. Your potential is not determined by whether you can see the fine print of a book, walk across the street or lift heavy objects with both hands. Your potential is not destroyed because your mother is an alcoholic, your father's a junkie or you have no parents at all. There are many people in wheelchairs who have given up. There are many people who come from the wrong side of town or a bad family situation who have given up. Don't be one of them. Beat the odds.

DEMAND SOMETHING OF YOUR POTENTIAL

If the Lord delights in a man's way, He makes his steps firm; though he stumble, he will not fall, for the Lord upholds him with His hand.
—PSALM 37:23-24

No one can climb beyond the limitations he has placed on himself. Success is never final—failure is never fatal. It is courage that counts—courage and the willingness to move on. A great deal of talent is lost to the world for want of a little courage. Every day sends to the grave, obscure men, whom fear and timidity have prevented from making their first attempt to do something. Never tell a person that something can't be done, because God may have been waiting for centuries for someone ignorant enough to believe that the impossible could be possible.

Success is never final—failure is never fatal.

The poorest of men are men without a dream. Don't be so afraid of failure that you refuse to try. Demand something of yourself. Failure is only an incident. There's more than the failure—there's success deep behind that failure. Failure is the opportunity to more intelligently begin again. When you fail, that is a great chance to start again. Learn from it and move on. Don't be paralyzed by the failure.

One good thing about failure is that it is proof that you tried. The greatest mistake you can make is to be afraid of making one.

People who do nothing in life are usually people who do nothing. People who don't make mistakes in life are usually people who didn't have a chance to make any because they never tried. Challenge your potential. Demand things of yourself that are beyond what you have already done. Expect more from yourself than the accomplishments that are easily within your reach. What you have is not all you are. The limit of your potential is God. It is better to attempt a thing and fail, than to never try and not know you could succeed.

I AM THE TRUE VINE

I am the true vine, and my Father is the gardener.
—JOHN 15:1

As a plant cannot fulfill its potential without being in relationship with the soil, so you cannot fulfill your true potential without being related to God. Thus Jesus says in the Book of John: "*I am the true vine*" (John 15:1). Jesus calls Himself the *true vine* because there are a lot of other vines around to get hooked into: education, philosophy, science, even religion.

The word vine here literally means "source of life." Like the grapevine for its branches, Jesus is our Source of life. If you depend on education, all you are going to have is what education can offer—an intellectual stimulation. No matter how many degrees you get, you are living below your potential because you are feeding on a false vine. You will never know your true information capacity if you are stuck on education. There are people who have been out of school for 50 years who don't know any more now than they knew when they were in school. Jesus says, "I am the True Vine." By this statement He implies that there are vines or sources that are not genuine.

The potential of the branches and the vine needs the attention of the gardener. The gardener works in the vineyard trying to bring as much life as possible out of the vines. Often he prunes the vines because he knows there is more life down in the roots. Since he is aware that he isn't getting the full capacity of the vine, he begins to clip some of the branches. Cutting off the old leaves that stop the vine from producing its full potential, the gardener starts to clean up the vine.

Are there some old leaves in your life that have been hanging around for five, ten or fifteen years? Do you need to quit a habit or two so your life more truly reflects the potential of the One who made you? Are you wasting time planning, setting up, committing and feeling guilty about sin? How many hours in a day are you losing to disobedience and rebellion? Prune your life through discipline and obedience to God, who desires your potential to be maximized. Remember, all God's commands and laws are given to maximize your performance and free your potential.

THE DISRUPTION OF THE GARDEN ENVIRONMENT

The eye is the lamp of the body. If your eyes are good, your whole body will be full of light. But if your eyes are bad, your whole body will be full of darkness.
—MATTHEW 6:22-23

Our present world is designed to destroy your potential. This attack on your environment has been around since Adam and Eve experienced similar pressures in the Garden.

Satan's attack came as mental pollution: "Did God really say…?" When the woman repeated what God had said, the serpent went one step further to devastate the woman's faith in God and His words:

> *"You will not surely die," the serpent said to the woman. "For God knows that when you eat of it your eyes will be opened, and you will be like God, knowing good and evil"* (Genesis 3:4-5).

Thus, the serpent completely undermined the woman's faith in God. The progression of the corruption that controlled Eve also seeks to ensnare you.

Pollution starts with the eyes. Seeing isn't sinning, and looking won't kill you. Seeing is the opening through which sinful thoughts and actions begin to take hold. If you don't want to eat, don't look.

> *When the woman saw that the fruit of the tree was...pleasing to the eye...* (Genesis 3:6).

Your trouble deepens when you move from considering the right or wrong of your action to an analysis of the relative merit of what you want. This is particularly true if your good doesn't equal God's good.

Desire pollutes the environment because it makes you want something at any expense. Your eyes get cloudy and your vision becomes blurred until everything looks right, even though it may be wrong. When desire makes you crave what you want no matter what the consequences, sit tight. You may grab something that will burn you!

Sin enters your life when your environment becomes so corrupt that you disobey God's commands and experience the brokenness that follows your disobedience. Suddenly you're in a mess and you're on your own. You no longer have a relationship with God that allows you to rely on His power and wisdom to deal with your problems. That's when your sanity starts to go. That's when pain and heartache fill your days. God doesn't have to convict you of sin because the polluted atmosphere of guilt and excuses will.

Live Effectively

I can do everything through Him who gives me strength.
—Philippians 4:13

I am trying to help you become aware of the great treasure you possess, which is your potential. I have addressed millions of people on this issue of living effectively. Repeatedly I have stressed that it is better to have never been born than to live and not fulfill the purpose for which you were given life. This truth is echoed in Ecclesiastes 6:3-5.

> *A man may have a hundred children and live many years; yet no matter how long he lives, if he cannot enjoy his prosperity and does not receive proper burial, I say that a stillborn child is better off than he. It comes without meaning, it departs in darkness, and in darkness its name is shrouded. Though it never saw the sun or knew anything, it has more rest than does that man.*

This passage asserts that it would be better for an individual never to have been born than for him to live on this planet many years and not fulfill the purpose for which God gave him birth. In essence, when you become aware of the tremendous potential that resides within you, you are obligated to release that wealth to the world around you.

YOUR POTENTIAL BENEFITS THE FUTURE

...consider well her ramparts, view her citadels,
that you may tell of them to the next generation.
—PSALM 48:13

God gave you the wealth of your potential—your abilities, gifts, talents, energies, creativity, ideas, aspirations, and desires—for the blessing of future generations. You bear the responsibility to activate, release, and deposit them. This generational principle of God, the Father of creation, is crucial to your full appreciation of the principle of potential. Tragedy strikes whenever a person fails to die empty.

I wonder how many hundreds of people—perhaps thousands or millions—were born or are yet to be born who need to benefit from the books you have neglected to write, the songs you have failed to compose, or the invention you have continued to postpone. Perhaps there are millions who need the ministry you have yet to begin or the business venture you have not yet started.

The next generation needs the treasure of your potential. Think of the many inventions, books, songs, works of art, and great accomplishments others in past generations have left for you. Even as their treasures have become your blessings, so your treasures must become your children's unborn children's blessings. You must not die unfinished and let the grave steal the gems of the future. Deliver your potential to inspire the children of our world to release theirs.

THE MAXIMUM OF MEDIOCRITY

Arise, shine, for your light has come, and
the glory of the Lord rises upon you.
—ISAIAH 60:1

What does it mean to maximize? What is maximum? The word *maximum* may be defined as "supreme, greatest, highest, and ultimate." It is synonymous with such concepts as pinnacle, preeminence, culmination, apex, peak, and summit. It implies the highest degree possible. Just a brief look at these concepts immediately convicts us of the many opportunities we have abused and forfeited because we have failed or have refused to give our all.

This failure to do our best, to go beyond the expectations of others, to express ourselves fully, to live up to our true potential, to extend ourselves to the limit of our abilities, to give it all we have, to satisfy our own convictions, is called *mediocrity*. Simply put, *mediocrity* is living below our known, true potential. It is accepting the norm, pleasing the status quo, and doing what we can get by with. Therefore, to *maximize* is to express, expose, experience, and execute all the hidden, God-given abilities, talents, gifts, and potential through God's vision breathed in our souls to fulfill His purpose for our lives on earth.

How tragic that most of the nearly six billion people on this planet will settle for an average life limited only by their unwillingness to extend themselves to the summit of their own selves. Anything less than maximum is mediocrity. In other words, *mediocrity* may be defined as the region of our lives bounded on the north by compromise, on the south by indecision, on the east by past thinking, and on the west by a lack of vision. Mediocrity is the spirit of the average, the anthem of the norm, and the heart-beat of the ordinary. Mediocrity is so common and pervasive that those who are labeled as genius or exceptional have to do only a little extra.

Remember, we were created to be above average, unnormal, and extraordinary. God never intended for success in our lives to be measured by the opinion of others or the standards set by the society in which we live. In fact, the Scriptures instruct us *not* to "*conform any longer to the pattern* [standards] *of this world, but* [to] *be transformed by the renewing of* [our] *mind*" (Romans 12:2). To maximize ourselves, we will find it necessary to declare independence from the world of the norm and to resist the gravity of the average in order to enjoy the outer limits of the new frontiers of our abilities. Why do so many of us settle for mediocrity? The answer is found in what I call the curse of comparison.

DISSATISFACTION WITH A FRACTION

...for it is God who works in you to will and to act according to His good purpose.
—PHILIPPIANS 2:13

One of life's great tragedies is that the majority of the world's population is composed of individuals who have negotiated an agreement with mediocrity, signed a contract with the average, and pledged allegiance to the ordinary. They have resolved never to be more than society has made them or do more than is expected. What a tragedy of destiny. God expects more!

Inside of every human being is a deep call of destiny to do something worthwhile with our lives. The urge to accomplish great things and engage in significant endeavors is the germ of purpose planted by God in the heart of man. Why then do we settle for so little? Why do we abandon our dreams and deny our purpose? Why do we live below our privilege, buried in the cemetery of wishful thinking and empty regrets?

As we have seen, one reason we fail to progress in fulfilling our purpose is satisfaction with our present measure of success. The belief that we have arrived is the deterrent that keeps us from getting to our destination. A second part of the answer lies in the fact that we have accepted the present state of our lives as the best we can do under the circumstances.

Prepare to Overcome Satan's Attack

Put on the full armor of God so that you can take your stand against the devil's schemes.
—Ephesians 6:11

We need to learn how to defend our potential. *One way you can prepare to defend your potential is to make wise choices.* Consider carefully with whom you associate and where you spend your time. Examine your reading material and how you fill your day. Be cautious with whom you share your dreams—if you share them at all.

A second priority in preparing to meet satan's attack is to be sure that your vision is from God. Don't conjure up your own ideas. If they contradict God's Word, you know your ideas are not from Him. God will not deny His Word. False dreams and fake prophecies are sure ways to lose your potential. Satan will distract you any way he can. Prepare for his attack by staying in close fellowship with God and by seeking His knowledge and wisdom.

A third method for fortifying yourself against the assault of evil is to seek God's discipline and direction in your life. Be truthful in your dealings. Act with justice and virtue. Live at peace with others in so far as it is within your power, being careful, however, not to compromise your loyalty and obedience to God and His Word. Seek His chastening when you have failed and "*rejoice in* [your] *sufferings, because... suffering produces perseverance; perseverance, character; and character, hope. And hope does not disappoint us...*" (Romans 5:3-5). God will honor your efforts to obey Him and, in so doing, you will guard your potential.

Sooner or later, satan is going to step over the boundaries of your defense and you are going to be under attack. Then it is time to move from *guarding* your potential to *protecting* it. Paul admonished the Ephesians to stand their ground and, after doing everything else, still to stand. Perseverance is the key. You may not win the war in one battle, but you can stand firm in the midst of each assault.

Abraham, Joseph, Moses, David, Paul—all persevered through numerous battles to emerge victorious. At times they faltered and failed, but they always returned to the battle. You too must persevere when the forces of evil threaten to overwhelm you to destroy your potential. The story of Nehemiah offers some hints on how to do this.

Uncapping the Well

But when He, the Spirit of truth, comes, He will guide you into all truth. He will not speak on His own; He will speak only what He hears, and He will tell you what is yet to come.
—John 16:13

Satan is the destroyer who comes to kill and steal and destroy. No one in the world stifles and clogs up and caps your potential like the devil does. He comes with a scheme to make you believe you can be nothing more than you have already seen. Jesus came to destroy this scheme. He came to unclog you and show you your true self. He's the best destroyer I know. I love this destroyer.

> *He who does what is sinful is of the devil, because the devil has been sinning from the beginning. The reason the Son of God appeared was to destroy the devil's work* (1 John 3:8).

First John 3:8 says that Jesus came into the world *to destroy* the works of the devil. The work of the devil is to kill and steal and destroy—he delights in capping off our potential. The work of Jesus is to tear off the cap—opening up what satan closed. Jesus came to do exactly the opposite of what satan has done. Jesus came, not to convince God of anything, but to convince us about who we really are. His job is to put us back in touch with what God put within us at birth.

DESTRUCTION DESTROYED

[Christ] who gave himself for our sins to rescue us from the present evil age, according to the will of our God and Father.
—GALATIANS 1:4

Scientists in the field of human potential have estimated that we use as little as ten percent of our abilities. Ninety percent of our capacities lie dormant and wasted. It is sad that we use only a small part of our abilities and talents. Most of us have no idea how much talent and potential we possess.

The work of the devil is to kill and steal and destroy—he delights up capping off our potential. But 1 John 3:8 says, "*The reason the Son of God appeared was to destroy the devil's work.*"

What does it mean to destroy the works of the devil? How does Jesus do His job? Jesus reverses what satan has done. Whatever Jesus undoes, satan did. Whatever works Jesus does, satan undid it first.

For example, when Jesus took sickness from a person's body, He undid the works of the devil. Thus the work of the devil was to put the sickness into that body. When Jesus took away our sins, He destroyed the devil's work of convincing us to sin. If Jesus fed hungry people, then it must mean that satan brings poverty and hunger. If Jesus opened the eyes of the blind, then satan must close them. Jesus came to destroy the works of the devil. Whatever He did destroyed satan's previous works. Thus when Jesus says, "Everything is possible if you'll just believe" (see Mark 9:23), He is reversing the lies satan has fed us. Jesus came to destroy satan's destruction.

YOUR PAST AND YOUR POTENTIAL

Create in me a pure heart, O God, and renew a steadfast spirit within me. ...Restore to me the joy of Your salvation and grant me a willing spirit, to sustain me.
—PSALM 51:10,12

A step in recovering potential is the ability to move beyond your past and to use it to inform and improve your future. All of us have things in our pasts of which we are ashamed. While self-forgiveness takes away the sting of those confessed sins, it does not remove from our minds the memory of those wrongs. We must learn to live with our memories and allow them to be a positive force in our lives.

King David, after his sin with Bathsheba, most certainly was haunted by his wrong (see 2 Samuel 11:1–12:25). Overwhelmed by the enormity of his sin, he could have forfeited his potential to serve God as the king of God's people. Instead, David confessed his sin (see 2 Samuel 12:13 and Psalm 51) and petitioned God. Today David is remembered as a man after God's heart and the greatest king in the history of God's people.

This same restorative power of God can move you beyond the negative opinions, poor judgments, unhealthy relationships, detrimental environments, and adverse circumstances of your past. No sin is too great for God to forgive. No relationship is beyond His restoration. His transforming power can redirect your misguided and harmful actions and enable you to remove yourself from the destructive environments and crippling circumstances that threaten your potential. No memory is too deep for Him to heal. No problem is beyond His blessing and power.

The key to moving beyond all that haunts you from your past is allowing those memories to empower you instead of destroy you. For example, if you were addicted to drugs and you know firsthand the destructive forces they unleash, use your experiences to help those who are at risk today of experiencing the same pain you've survived.

Discouraging, defeating experiences may be part of your past life, but there is no reason why they must continue to discourage and defeat you. Indeed, they can become stepping stones to the releasing and maximizing of your potential if you are willing to acknowledge your past, to learn from your mistakes, and to allow God's transforming power to turn your loss into gain. With God's help, you are capable of rising above your shortcomings and of redeeming your less than perfect decisions. He has not given up on you. He's waiting to see what you will do with the rest of your life. Protect the present and the future from the past by facing the past and moving beyond it. This is an essential element of the journey to recover your potential.

God Offers You a Rewrite

You hem me in—behind and before; you have laid your hand upon me
—Psalm 139:5

God wants to take you back to the beginning, because His plans far outreach your plans. His design for your life is so great that King David describes it as *vast* (see Psalm 139:17). You are thinking about being a teacher while God wants you to open a school. You have plans to be a clerk while God wants you to own the store. You want to work in a neighboring town while God wants you to go to Africa. You often cheat yourself because you don't realize the potential you have. Why settle to be a doorman when God wants you to own the house? David says it this way: "God, when I look at your thoughts in the book on me, it's like all the sands in the ocean. Your thoughts are endless. I can't fathom your confidence in me."

God designed you to live out the careful plans He prepared for you. You are made in God's image. The plan He wrote for you is perfect and right. No detail or part is missing. You have the potential to live out all that God has planned for your life—but only if you accept Jesus Christ as your Savior and Lord. That's the first step toward understanding why you were born.

Though you've messed up God's perfect plan for your life, He graciously offers to write another book for you. It probably won't be the best seller the first book was designed to be, but at least God gives you the chance to start over. He comes and puts you back in chapter one so you can live the many details of His plan. That's what being born again is all about. It's the opportunity to start over—it's finally getting back to the first chapter of God's book on you. God has great plans for you—that's why He gave you life. Self-acceptance is the key to healthy self-esteem.

Accept yourself as God made you. Allow His power to transform your weakness, rather than belittling yourself when you make mistakes.

ABOUT MYLES MUNROE

DR. MYLES MUNROE was a beloved statesman and internationally renowned bestselling author, lecturer, life coach, and government consultant. His legacy continues to impact countless lives—individually launching people into lives of discovered purpose and unlocked potential, and corporately ushering the global church into a greater revelation of demonstrating the Kingdom of God. He, along with his wife, Ruth Ann, served as senior pastors of Bahamas Faith Ministries International Fellowship. They have two children, Charisa and Chairo.